Introduction

The Affidavit

The Search Warrant: Basic Elements

The Search Warrant: People

The Search Warrant: Computers and Internet Service Providers

The Search Warrant: Child Pornography

The Search Warrant: Property Crimes, Fraud, and Forgery

The Search Warrant: Narcotics and Gangs

The Search Warrant: Special Procedures

<u>Waiver of Knock Notice Requirement-Affidavit</u>

<u>Waiver of Knock Notice Requirement-Affidavit</u>

Introduction

One of the main challenges encountered by many law enforcement officers when drafting a search warrant is properly describing the person, place, or thing to be searched, and describing the reason for searching for associated evidence. Most law enforcement officers recognize the need to search for and seize common items of contraband such as narcotics and weapons. But what if the evidence or contraband you are searching for doesn't fall within the investigators experience? What if no one at the agency has ever written a search warrant for a particular crime or drug? The purpose of this manual is to fill that gap and give law enforcement officers examples of search warrant and/or affidavit language which has been used successfully in the past.

Neither the author nor the publishers are attorneys. It is strongly recommended that you seek the advice and assistance of a prosecuting attorney when writing a search warrant.

Why Get a Warrant?

Search warrants are one of the most valuable tools available to law enforcement officers. The process of obtaining a search warrant outweighs the time and effort necessary to complete the process. The courts have consistently emphasized their preference for searches made with a search warrant versus other types of searches such as consent, exigent circumstances, and searches incident to arrest and current case law makes it extremely difficult for a suspect to prevent the admission of evidence seized pursuant to a search warrant. In fact, the United States Supreme Court case US v. Ventresca (1965) 380 U.S. 102 108-9 has frequently been cited by appellate courts in ruling on the validity of search warrants:

"If the teachings of the Court's cases are to be followed and the constitutional policy served, affidavits for search warrants . . . must be tested and interpreted by magistrates and courts in a common-sense and realistic fashion. They are normally drafted by non-lawyers in the midst and haste of a criminal investigation. Technical requirements of elaborate specificity once exacted under common law pleadings have no proper place in this area. A grudging or negative attitude by reviewing courts toward warrants will tend to discourage police officers from submitting their evidence to a judicial officer before acting.

This is not to say that probable cause can be made out by affidavits which are purely conclusory, stating only the affiant's or an informer's belief that probable cause exists without detailing any of the "underlying circumstances" upon which that belief is based. Recital of some of the underlying circumstances in the affidavit is essential if the magistrate is to perform his detached function and not serve merely as a rubber stamp for the police. However, where these circumstances are detailed, where reason for crediting the source of the information is given, and when a magistrate has found probable cause, the courts should not invalidate the warrant by interpreting the affidavit in a hyper technical, rather than a common sense, manner. Although in a particular case it may not be easy to determine when an affidavit demonstrates the existence of probable cause, the resolution of doubtful or marginal cases in this area should be largely determined by the preference to be accorded to warrants."

What Is A Search Warrant?

"A search warrant is an order in writing, in the name of the people, signed by a magistrate, directed to a peace officer, commanding him or her to search for a person or persons, a thing or things, or personal property, and, in the case of a thing or things or personal property, bring the same before the magistrate". (California Penal Code section 1523.).

When Can A Search Warrant Be Issued?

According to California Penal Code 1524 a search warrant may be issued in the following situations:

(1) When the property was stolen or embezzled.

(2) When the property or things were used as the means of committing a felony.

(3) When the property or things are in the possession of any person with the intent to use them as a means of committing a public offense, or in the possession of another to whom he or she may have delivered them for the purpose of concealing them or preventing their being discovered.

(4) When the property or things to be seized consist of any item or constitute any evidence that tends to show a felony has been committed, or tends to show that a particular person has committed a felony.

(5) When the property or things to be seized consist of evidence that tends to show that sexual exploitation of a child, in violation of Section 311.3, or possession of matter depicting sexual conduct of a person under the age of 18 years, in violation of Section 311.11., has occurred or is occurring.

(6) When there is a warrant to arrest a person.

(7) When a provider of electronic communication service or remote computing service has records or evidence, as specified in Section 1524.3, showing that property was stolen or embezzled constituting a misdemeanor, or that property or things are in the possession of any person with the intent to use them as a means of committing a misdemeanor public offense, or in the possession of another to whom he or she may have delivered them for the purpose of concealing them or preventing their discovery."

(8) When the property or things to be seized include an item or any evidence that tends to show a violation of Section 3700.5 of the Labor Code, or tends to show that a particular person has violated Section

3700.5 of the Labor Code.

(9) When the property or things to be seized include a firearm or any other deadly weapon at the scene of, or at the premises occupied or under the control of the person arrested in connection with, a domestic violence incident involving a threat to human life or a physical assault as provided in subdivision (b) of Section 12028.5.

(10) When the property or things to be seized include a firearm or any other deadly weapon that is owned by, or in the possession of, or in the custody or control of, a person described in subdivision (a) of Section 8102 of the Welfare and Institutions Code.

(11) When the property or things to be seized include a firearm that is owned by, or in the possession of, or in the custody or control of, a person who is subject to the prohibitions regarding firearms pursuant to Section 6389 of the Family Code, if a prohibited firearm is possessed, owned, in the custody of, or controlled by a person against whom a protective order has been issued pursuant to Section 6218 of the Family Code, the person has been lawfully served with that order, and the person has failed to relinquish the firearm as required by law.

The Affidavit

Search Warrant Affidavits

An affidavit is a statement made under penalty of perjury before a magistrate. According to California Penal Code section 1525: "A search warrant cannot be issued but upon probable cause, supported by affidavit, naming or describing the person to be searched or searched for, and particularly describing the property, thing, or things and the place to be searched." Per Penal Code section 1527: "The affidavit or affidavits must set forth the facts tending to establish the grounds of the application, or probable cause for believing that they exist."

The law enforcement officer seeking the search warrant is known as the affiant. The affiant must present facts to the magistrate establishing probable cause for the seizure of specific items at a particular described location. The United States Supreme Court has declared probable cause in relation to search warrants as "The task of the issuing magistrate is simply to make a practical common-sense decision whether, given all the circumstances set forth in the affidavit before him, including the 'veracity' and 'basis of knowledge' of persons supplying hearsay information, there in a _fair probability_ that contraband or evidence of a crime will be found in a particular place."

It is important to note that this does not mean there is a guarantee or absolute certainty that evidence or contraband will be found at the location of the search warrant. Instead, it is merely likely that evidence or contraband will be found.

Similar to a police report, a search warrant affidavit is usually written in a chronological and narrative format. If you have written a police report, you already have the basic underlying skills to write a search warrant affidavit. There is nothing strange or magical in the writing of a search warrant but there are several elements which must be met in order for the affidavit to withstand the scrutiny of the courts both during the initial review and subsequent examination during criminal proceedings.

The affidavit should include all of the information the affiant has, including their personal observations, official sources of information, and what he/she has been told by others. Officers do not need to attempt to write like attorneys and simple declarations are best. There is no need to dress up the affidavit with 'hereto with' and 'in accordance with'.

Writing styles are different between jurisdictions. Some areas prefer their affidavits be written in the third person past tense such as "Your affiant went to the scene of the crime..." versus "I went to the scene of the crime..." There is no absolute legal standard about how the affidavit should be constructed and law enforcement officers should use the standard their prosecutors support. However, it is usually easier and more natural to write in the first person.

The affidavit usually begins documentation of the affiant's training and experience, commonly referred to as a 'hero sheet'. Documentation of specific training and experience allows an officer to make conclusions based on the information in the affidavit which might not be available to another officer without the same training and experience. The lack of expertise in a particular subject does not invalidate an officer's ability to seek a search warrant. However, it is important to remember that a law enforcement officer's basic training and patrol experiences can be sufficient to establish expertise as long as they are properly documented. Some methods of documenting this can include:

Stating the name of the law enforcement agency you are currently employed by, your current assignment, and when you began working for them.

"I am you affiant, Officer Sean Gauge with the River City Police Department (RCPD) and have been employed by them since February 2000. I am currently assigned to the Patrol Division."

List any other law enforcement agencies you have worked for and how long you were employed by them.

"Prior to my employment with RCPD I worked was employed by the Freedom Police Department as a Police Officer from January 1998- February 2000."

"I graduated from the Freedom Police Department Basic Academy in January 1998."

"I have taken the following law enforcement training classes: Basic Narcotics Investigations March 1999, Street Level Narcotics Sales November 1999, Drug Abuse Recognition May 2001, Advanced Narcotics

Investigations, March 2002…"

[NOTE: There is a tendency in some affidavits to list every training class the affiant has ever taken. Unless your expertise as an Emergency Vehicle Operator Instructor is relevant to the crime under investigation, leave it out. Similarly, there is reluctance on the part on newer or inexperienced officers to believe the lack of specialized training precludes them from being the affiant. This is not true. It may limit your ability to render an opinion regarding the relevance of certain information or evidence but it does not mean you cannot write the affidavit.]

List any relevant special assignments you have had which bolster your expertise regarding the crime under investigation. List the dates the assignment lasted.

"I was assigned to the RCPD's Gang Enforcement Team from June 2004 until July 2008."

Document an approximation of the total number of similar investigations and/or arrests you have performed or participated in during your career as a law enforcement officer. This can include cases where you were not necessarily the primary investigating or arresting officer, but where you actively participated in or witnessed the location and collection of evidence and interviews with defendants and witnesses. This can be used to supplement formal training in a particular area.

"I have participated in no less than 100 investigations involving being under the influence of, possession of, possession for sales, and transportation for sales of narcotics and other drugs such as methamphetamine, cocaine, heroin, MDMA, marijuana, and prescription medications."

If you have been the affiant in other search warrants or participated in the preparation, service, or execution of a search warrant(s), you may also choose to document this in the affidavit.

"I have assisted with the execution of approximately 20 search warrants resulting in the seizure of contraband and evidence."

You may also choose to list any relevant education, training, and experience which you believe enhances your expertise relative to the crime under investigation.

"I have a Bachelor of Science degree in Administration of Justice from San Jose State University."

"I served for four years in the United States Army as a Military Police Officer."

"Prior to my employment as a Police Officer I worked as a Loss Prevention Agent for Major Department Store."

Incorporating Information into the Affidavit and Search Warrant

Sometimes the information in a search warrant affidavit comes from a combination of sources. Personal observations of the officer, information obtained from other law enforcement officers from the same or different agency, official sources of information such as the Department of Motor Vehicles, witnesses, and informants. You can't take anything for granted when writing your search warrant affidavit and it is important to properly document all of the relevant sources of information used to formulate the opinion that there is probable cause to believe there is evidence or contraband in a particular location.

Some jurisdictions attach police reports to the affidavit whereas others consider the reference to the report in the affidavit sufficient. The following is an example of language used to include a crime report into an affidavit:

Crime Reports-Affidavit

Your Affiant has received and read an official River City Police Department Report, (Report number), consisting of (pages) pages, which is attached hereto as Exhibit No. (exhibit number) and incorporated as if fully set forth herein. Acting upon the information contained within this exhibit, your Affiant and his fellow officers conducted an investigation as set forth in the (number of pages) page(s) River City Police Departments Investigator's Report which is attached hereto and incorporated as if fully set forth herein as Exhibit No. (exhibit number).

Witnesses and Informants

Information received from citizens frequently initiate, or forms the basis, for many search warrants. The courts have held there are two primary types of people who provide information to law enforcement; witnesses who are citizen informants, and those that are criminal informants who are providing information to law enforcement for compensation or case consideration.

The motivations of these two different types of informants are different and are afforded varying credibility by the courts. Citizen informants who are not involved with criminal activity and volunteer their information for the good of society are commonly held to a lower threshold to establish their reliability versus those who are involved in criminal activity and receive some form of compensation of consideration for their information.

Because these two distinct categories of informants are treated differently by the courts, they need to be addressed differently in a search warrant affidavit.

In documenting information received from a citizen informant in an affidavit, it is not necessary to disclose their name. However, the affiant must establish some facts to show the magistrate that the informant was actually a citizen informant and was not operating as an untested police informant or confidential informant.

Citizen Informant-Affidavit

Based upon your Affiant's training, experience and conversations that your Affiant had with other Law Enforcement Officers and/or reports that your Affiant has read, your Affiant knows that the informant is a citizen informant because the informant was neither under arrest nor a suspect in any crime. The informant stated that he/she gave the information to help the police. The informant appeared to be a citizen acting in the interest of law enforcement and for no other reason.

Confidential informants are commonly categorized into two classes, untested and reliable. Untested informants are those whose reliability has not been established. Reliable informants are those who have provided information in the past which was used to assist in establishing probable cause for a search warrant which resulted in the seizure of evidence or contraband or whose information has led to the arrest to criminal suspects. Different jurisdictions have different standards for what constitutes a reliable informant and it is best to check with the appropriate prosecutors' office in your area. It is important to note information received from an untested informant, who does not meet the standards of a citizen informants, is not considered reliable by itself. However, if the information can be corroborated by other facts indicating that reliance on the information is reason, it can be considered reliable. In other words, a valid search warrant may be issued based on information received from an untested informant if that information can be corroborated via other means.

Reliable Informant-Affidavit

Based upon your Affiant's training, experience and conversations that your Affiant had with other Law Enforcement Officers and/or reports that your Affiant has read, your Affiant knows the Informant to be reliable because the Informant gave your Affiant information on (number) prior occasion(s) within the past (number) months which proved to be accurate and resulted in the arrest and conviction of (number) person(s) for (type of crimes). Your Affiant does not wish to give further details as to past information provided by this Informant for fear it will furnish clues to his/her identity.

Protecting Informants Identity-Affidavit

Based upon your Affiant's training, experience and conversations that your Affiant had with other Law Enforcement Officers and/or reports that your Affiant has read, your Affiant knows that it is necessary to keep the identity of this Informant confidential because your Affiant believes disclosure of his/her identity would impair his/her future usefulness to Law Enforcement Officers and endanger the Informant's life.

The Search Warrant: Basic Elements

Dominion and Control Evidence-Search Warrant

There are some items which are standard in most search warrants. Evidence of dominion and control is one of the first things listed in most search warrants. This type of evidence is useful in linking the suspect(s) to the evidence or contraband. Dominion and control evidence usually consists of things like documents, records, and keys. Common examples of dominion and control evidence sought in search warrants are:

Any items tending to establish the identity of persons who have dominion and control of the location, premises, automobiles, or items to be seized, including delivered mail, whether inside the location or in the mail box/s, bills, utility bills, telephone bills, miscellaneous addressed mail, personal letters, personal identification, purchase receipts, rent receipts, sales receipts, tax statements, payroll check stubs, keys and receipts for safe deposit box(s), keys and receipts for rental storage space, keys and receipts for post office box or mail drop rentals, ignition keys, car door and trunk keys, vehicle ownership certificates or "pink slips," and/or vehicle registration slips, recordation of voice transmissions on telephone answering machines, and photographs tending to show occupation of the residence / business and connection between co-conspirators, whether identified, or unidentified, Any examples of handwriting including letters, address books, business records, canceled checks, notes, and/or lists.

Dominion and Control Evidence-Affidavit

Based upon your Affiant's training, experience and conversations that your Affiant had with other Law Enforcement Officers and/or reports that your Affiant has read, your Affiant knows that during the service of this Search Warrant there are many articles of personal and/or business property tending to establish the identity of persons who have dominion and control over the premises, business, vehicles, and/or items to be seized. Your Affiant believes that these items will tend to connect the premises, locations, persons, and vehicles to be searched with the items to be seized and the case being investigated. It is your Affiant's opinion that these types of items are usually present at the location sought to be searched by this Search Warrant and that they will therefore likely still be found in the location, and/or the person to be searched.

Videotape, Photograph, Digital Image during Search Warrant Service-Search Warrant

Some jurisdictions choose to include specific authorization to take video, photographs, or digital images during the execution of the search warrant. Similarly, some law enforcement officers choose to include specific authorization to take measurements and seizure other forensic evidence. While there is not specific requirement to do so, it is a recommended practice in almost every search warrant execution to take images before and after a search to preclude the suspect(s) from claiming damage by searching law enforcement officers.   For those officers who choose to add specific authorization to take video, photos, or digital images during a warrant service, the following language can be incorporated:

Peace Officers or assigned representatives are authorized, during the execution of this Search Warrant, to video tape, photograph and/or take digital images, at the discretion of the Searching Officers, inside and outside of the location, any and all items and/or vehicles at the location, in addition, can identify and photograph and/or digital image all persons present at the Search Warrant location during the period of execution of this Search Warrant.

Videotape, Photograph, Digital Image during Search Warrant Service-Search Warrant-Affidavit

Based upon your Affiant's training, experience and conversations that your Affiant had with other Law Enforcement Officers and/or reports that your Affiant has read, your Affiant knows that Peace Officer(s) or assigned representative(s) should videotape, photograph and/or digital image the location during the execution of this Search Warrant. The Affiant needs control of who takes the images. Computer(s) may be at the scene and may be operating during the service of the Search Warrant. The images on the computer(s) screens are transient, it may be necessary to videotape, photograph and/or digital image the computer monitor screen(s). Photographing of the location, vehicles and persons present at the scene is often helpful in the showing possession of the premises and evidence. It is also good to show the condition of the location as the Search Warrant is served and to show the condition of the location after the Search Warrant has been served.

Forensic - Photograph, Take Measurements, Seize Weapons and Evidence-Search Warrant

Peace Officers or assigned representatives are authorized, during the execution of this Search Warrant, to video tape, photograph, and/or take digital images of the scene and surrounding area(s), take measurements and make sketches of the scene and adjacent areas; and to seize weapons, bludgeons, and guns; suspected blood and other physiological fluids; hair and fibers; fingerprints, footprints, and other impressions left at the (type of crime) scene; gunshot residue; any and all instruments used to aid and abet in the commission of (type of crime), clothing of the suspects(s) and/or victims(s); photos and film, developed and undeveloped; samples of paint, glass, and other fluids and solids that may have stained or adhered to the clothing and person of the victim(s) and/or suspect(s).

Forensic - Photograph, Take Measurements, Seize Weapons & Evidence-Affidavit

Based upon your Affiant's training, experience and conversations that your Affiant had with other Law Enforcement Officers and/or reports that your Affiant has read, your Affiant knows that Peace Officer(s) or assigned representative(s) should videotape, photograph, and/or take digital images of the scene and surrounding areas during the service of this Search Warrant. The Peace Officer(s) or representative needs to take measurements and make sketches of the scene and adjacent areas; and seize weapons, bludgeons, and/or guns. They need to take suspected blood and other physiological fluids; hair and fibers; fingerprints, footprints, and other impressions left at the crime scene. Gunshot residue; any and all instruments used to aid and abet in the commission of crime need to be located and seized. Clothing of the suspects(s) and or victims(s); photos and film, developed and undeveloped; samples of paint, glass, and other fluids and solids that may have stained or adhered to the clothing and person of the victim(s) and/or suspect(s) need to be located and seized from the scene.

Homicide-Affidavit

Based upon your Affiant's training, experience and conversations that your Affiant had with other Law Enforcement Officers and/or reports that your Affiant has read, your Affiant believes that the location to be searched may contain evidence such as the murder weapon, blood samples, body tissues, human hair fibers, as well as, other written or taped documents which will identify the individual(s) responsible for these/this homicide(s). Your Affiant knows that due to the violent nature of this/these homicide(s), hair and blood evidence from the suspects and/or victim(s) may be present at the location of this Search Warrant.

Your Affiant may need to have forensic specialists for the location(s) to be searched, to aid in the search for trace evidence of blood, hair fibers, bodily fluids, body tissue and fingerprints at the location. Your Affiant requests permission to photograph the location and its contents. Your Affiant also requests permission to seize any personal photographs at the location that depict.

Homicide - Forensic - Photograph / Sketch / Evidence-Affidavit

Based upon your Affiant's training, experience and conversations that your Affiant had with other Law Enforcement Officers and/or reports that your Affiant has read, your Affiant requests to have the scene and surrounding area(s) photographed, videotaped and/or digital imaged; take measurements and make sketches of the scene and adjacent areas; seize weapons, knifes, bludgeons, guns, ropes, or other restraining devices; suspected blood and other physiological fluids; hair and fibers; fingerprints, footprints and other impressions left at the homicide scene; gunshot residue; expended and unexpended bullets, cartridge casings, waddings, and other projectiles; any and all instruments used to aid and assist in the commission of the homicide; clothing of the suspect(s) and or victim(s); photos and film, developed and undeveloped; written material and correspondence containing names, addresses, and phone numbers, of victim(s) and possible suspect(s) and witnesses; written material containing statements showing ill feelings, threats, and other possible motives between victim(s) and possible suspect(s); written material showing ownership or occupancy of building, structure, residence, room, or vehicle; samples of paint, glass, and other fluids and solids that may have stained or adhered to the clothing and person of the victim(s) and/or suspect(s); alcohol, narcotics, dangerous drugs, and other intoxicants, as well as, paraphernalia for the use or sale of the preceding, but not limited to, syringes, spoons, inhalers, roach clips, bottle caps, scales, balloons, condoms and/or cutting agents; cloth material such as, but not limited to, sheets, blankets, pillow cases, cushions, seat covers, etc.; objects or portions thereof having suspected bullet damage; any beer cans and/or bottles and/or similar objects.

Arson-Search Warrant

Any and all evidence related to the cause and origin of the fire which took place on 12/8/11, including flammable liquids, i.e. gasoline, kerosene, alcohol, lighter fluid, etc., combustible liquids, timing devices, candles , residue wax, liquid samples, chemicals capable of igniting or sustaining fire, materials to spread fire throughout the structure, i.e. trailers, evidence of removed property, evidence of altered property, electrical wiring samples, tampered fuse or circuit breakers, electrical outlet samples, extension cords, evidence supporting the condition of entrance and exit of building, charred wood samples, charred cloth samples, samples which support the approximate temperature of fire, i.e. metal samples which melted, substances capable of absorbing a flammable material, i.e. building materials.

Answer Telephone(s) during Search Warrant Service-Search Warrant

Many law enforcement officers incorporate specific language into their affidavits and search warrants authorized them to answer the suspect's phone if it received an incoming call during the execution of the warrant. For example:

Peace Officers during the execution of this Search Warrant may answer telephones and converse with callers at the location of this Search Warrant without revealing the Peace Officers true identity, and note and/or record any conversations and information received from the telephone calls, including caller identification information.

Answer Telephone(s) during Search Warrant Service-Affidavit

Based upon your Affiant's training, experience and conversations that your Affiant had with other Law Enforcement Officers and/or reports that your Affiant has read, it is your Affiant's opinion that the persons mentioned and other unknown persons are engaged in a conspiracy to commit felony crimes and that such persons often communicate with each other and coordinate their illegal activities by telephone. The searching officers should be able to answer any telephones in the location(s) to be searched and conceal their identities; as such conversations may constitute evidence of a felony and may identify other conspirators.

Weapons-Search Warrant

Any (handgun / pistol / revolver / rifle / shotgun / firearm / automatic weapon/caliber). In addition to any firearm, any spent (Caliber/Millimeter) casings, any miscellaneous gun/firearm pieces, ammunition, gun-cleaning items or kits, holsters, ammunition belts, original box packaging materials, (Clips/Magazines/Cylinders/Loading Devices), targets, expended pieces of lead/bullets, any photographs of firearms, or any paperwork showing the purchase, storage, disposition, and/or dominion and control over any guns, any ammunition, or any of the above items.

Weapons-Affidavit

Based upon your Affiant's training, experience and conversations that your Affiant had with other Law Enforcement Officers and/or reports that your Affiant has read, your Affiant requests to search for and seize any weapons, spent casings, any miscellaneous gun/firearm pieces, ammunition, gun-cleaning items or kits, holsters, ammunition belts, original box packaging materials, clips and/or magazines, targets, expended pieces of lead/bullets, any photographs of firearms, or any paperwork showing the purchase, storage, disposition, and/or dominion and control over any guns, any ammunition, or any of the above items.

Your Affiant believes that whether or not the firearm(s) sought are recovered, the above items would tend to show that a firearm(s) existed and may have once been located in a place to which the suspect had access, and that these items would tend to connect the suspect with the weapon(s) sought. The above items are not normally disposed of after the commission of a crime, and they are therefore still likely to be found in any location or vehicles to be searched, and/or on the person of any suspect to be searched pursuant to this Search Warrant.

The Search Warrant: Places to be Searched

Describing the places/items you are searching

California Penal Code section 1529 states the property, things, or persons to be searched must be described with "reasonable particularity." Descriptions must be accurate. An incorrect address or faulty description may invalidate a warrant. It is recommended that the affiant personally observe the person, place, item, or vehicle to be searched or to have another reliable law enforcement officer do so. A good general rule is that descriptions in a search warrant should be sufficiently particular so that another officer with no knowledge of the case were to serve the warrant, the other officer would have no problem locating the place, recognizing the vehicle, or identifying the person to be searched. Later sections of this book give examples of language used by other law enforcement officers to search for a variety of both common and uncommon evidence and contraband.

Places

Describing most places to be searched in an affidavit is relatively simple. However, it is not sufficient to simply state 123 Main Street. Remember to keep the following premise in mind: A law enforcement officer with no knowledge of the investigation should be able to pick it up and determine the location to be searched without question. The following are templates for use in describing places to be searched.

Single-Family Residence or a Duplex-Search Warrant

The following template is appropriate for residences, whether single or multi-story, including duplexes:

A _________________ -story residence located on the _____________ side of the street. _______________street runs in a ___________ direction. The closest cross street is _____________________, which runs in a _____________________ direction and is located to the ______________ of the residence. There is a (n) (detached\attached) (garage\carport) located on the _________ side of the residence. The residence has a _______________colored (brick\stucco\wood) exterior, with_______________ colored (brick\stucco\wood) trim and a _________________ roof. The ___________ colored numbers "_________________" are affixed to the __________ side of the structure and are located _________________________________ the numbers ____________ are stenciled in black, on a white background, on the curb in front of the residence; including all rooms, attics, basements, and other parts therein, the surrounding grounds and any garages, storage rooms, trash containers, and outbuildings of any kind located thereon.

Apartment House or Large Complex-Search Warrant

A multi-unit, apartment complex known as the _________________ apartment complex and located on the _____________ side of _______________ street. _________________ street runs in a _____________ direction. There are (detached\attached) (garages\carports) located on the _________ side of the (apartment house\complex). The closest cross street is _____________, which runs in a_____________direction and is located to the _________of the complex. The name (and street #s) _______________is/are located on a ____________ colored _____________ sign located on the _____________ side of the complex. The building containing apartment __________ is located in the _______________portion of the complex. The building has a _______________colored (brick\stucco\wood) exterior, with _____________ colored (brick\stucco\wood) trim and a _________________ roof. The building numbers _______________are located on the _______________side of the building. Apartment number _____________ is located on the _____________ level, and in the____________ portion of the building. the apartment numbers "_________________" are located _____________., including all rooms, attics, basements and other parts within apartment # ______and all garages, trash containers, and storage area designated for the use of apartment # _____, or for which keys to garages, trash containers, and storage area are found at the premises to be searched, or in the possession of the occupants of the premises.

Courtesy Mike Galli Deputy District Attorney Santa Clara County

Rural Locations-Address Unknown-Search Warrant

THE PREMISES to be searched consists of five adjacent lots/parcels located in an unincorporated area of Mendocino County, California, north of the town of Laytonville. These five parcels were identified using records at the Mendocino County Recorder's Office, and are recorded as being owned by "Carl Lyn." The lots are in hilly terrain in a rural, sparsely populated, undeveloped area of Mendocino County, described as: Mendocino County Assessor's Parcel Number (APN#) 064¬370-01; 064-370-02; 064-370-03; 064-370-04; 064-370-05. Located on these parcels are at least three structures including a brown-colored residence, gray-colored barn-like structure, and at least one small shed near the entrance to the property, and several vehicles parked in various places near the driveway/road.

Utilizing Goggle Mapping Systems/database, the main structure/residence was identified as having Global Positioning System (GPS) Latitude/Longitude approximate coordinates: N39 48 19.69, W123 28 17.91. These coordinates were verified by law enforcement equipped with a GPS device during the over-flight of the property described in the attached Affidavit.

The PREMISES can be reached by driving east from the intersection of U.S. Highway 101/Spyrock Road, north of Laytonville, California, approximately six miles to the intersection of Spyrock Road/Iron Peak Road, turning right onto Iron Peak Road and continuing in an easterly direction to the intersection of Iron Peak Road/Simmerly Road, turning left onto Simmerly Road and continuing to the intersection of Simmerly Road/Iron Creek Road, then continuing in a southeast direction on Iron Creek Road to the front gate, located on the west side of Iron Creek Road, that leads to the PREMISES to be searched. The GPS coordinates for the front gate of the PREMISES to be searched are approximately: N39 48 20.94, W123 28 18.80, which were verified by law enforcement personnel who drove to the entrance/gate area of this location on or about August 20, 2011.

See attached Exhibit A (copy of parcel map from Mendocino County Recorder's Office with boundary of the PREMISES drawn); Exhibit B (aerial image of the PREMISES obtained from Google Earth database, with GPS latitude and longitude coordinates); Exhibit C (an aerial photograph taken from above the PREMISES during the over flight of August 5, 2011, showing a portion of the PREMISES); Exhibit D (photograph of front gate/entrance to the PREMISES, taken on or about August 20, 2011).

Store or Business-Search Warrant

The name of the business, the address, and a brief description of its outer appearance should be stated.

THE PREMISES known as the "Joe's Coffee Shop" located at 123 Main Street, San Francisco CA, including all rooms, dining areas, service areas, kitchens, pantries, stoves, refrigerators, restrooms and other parts within the business including an office and any safe contained within the office in the rear of the premises, and any storage rooms, storage areas and trash containers, attached or unattached, located thereon. This location is a coffee shop on the first floor of a multi-story commercial building and the words, "Joe's Coffee Shop – Expensive Coffee Drinks a Specialty," appear in gold letters on the front window.

Business - Single Story Commercial Building-Search Warrant

THE PREMISES known as (name of business) located at (address), (city), California (zip code) described as a (type of business) in a (color & type of exterior) single-story commercial building and including all rooms, attics, service area, restrooms, lunch areas, lockers, storage areas, files, safes, and attached, or unattached trash areas and trash containers.

Residence or Business - Unknown Address-Search Warrant

If the specific address is unknown or the location is not marked with an address, special particularity should be used in describing it. These descriptions must be more detailed than those in which an address is known. This is because sufficient detail must be given to avoid any possibility that the description could apply to other nearby locations.

THE PREMISES described as a (number of stories) story building with a (color & type of exterior) exterior, a (type of roof) roof, and (color & type of trim) trim located on the (direction) side of (name of street) between (name of street) and (name of street) in (city of the location), California, (zip code); this location is the (# of buildings) building/s (direction) of the (direction of corner) corner of (name of street) and (name of street) (add anything distinguishing about the building on this line) and including all rooms, attics, basements, and other parts therein, including the surrounding grounds, and any garages, storage rooms, trash containers, or outbuildings of any kind located thereon.

Hidden Compartments or Hiding Places At or Within a Location-Search Warrant

If there is a known hidden compartment or hiding place at the location or vehicle to be searched, a description of that hidden compartment or hiding place should be specifically included in the description of the premises. Unfortunately, you must state how you know about the hiding place or hidden compartment. This may create problems if the information came from a confidential informant. Consider sealing the affidavit.

THE PREMISES known as Joe's Coffee located at 123 Main Street, San Francisco, California including all rooms, dining areas, service areas, kitchens, pantries, stoves, refrigerators, restrooms and other parts within the business including an office and any safe contained within the office in the rear of the premises, and any storage rooms, storage areas and trash containers, attached or unattached, located thereon. Officers are authorized to search the crawl space accessible from the main storeroom and to use reasonable means, including destructive or damaging measures, to recover any evidence contained therein.

General Business Records-Search Warrant

Depending on the investigation, certain types of businesses, particularly those that contain specific records, may require a more description of the items to be seized.

All books of accounts and accounting papers in the name of the defendant business, all journals and ledgers, all spread sheets and working papers, balance sheet accounts, income statement accounts, commercial and personal checking accounts, all original and canceled checks, deposit and withdrawals source documents, whether typed or handwritten, bank statements, bank reconciliations, payroll accounts, employee records, payroll vouchers and time cards, Forms W-2, W-4, W-9, 1099's, I-9, Individual (1040), partnership, (1065 & K-1), and corporate tax returns (1120), tax records and tax filings, Board of Equalization and Employment Development Department, documents showing title, ownership, or interest in any real or personal property, and business licenses and Articles of Incorporation

Auto Dealership-Search Warrant

All vehicle sales and vehicle maintenance records relating to (specify vehicle and VIN) in the name of the defendant including vehicle inventory sale folder, retail or wholesale, which identifies the vehicle by dealer assigned stock number and VIN, motor vehicle purchase order identifying the vehicle by dealer stock number and VIN, description of the vehicle, name, address, telephone number of the buyer/owner, signature of the buyer/owner, sales price, title, transfer doc., license fee, sales tax of the vehicle, Federal Truth in Lending statements, finance charges, total deferred payment price, statement of insurance, credit insurance, seller assisted loan, method of payment, down payment, trade-in description, trade-in value, payment refund policy, drivers license information, proof of financial responsibility, retail installment sales contract describing buyer/co-buyer, creditor/seller, description of the vehicle, VIN, use for purchase, Federal Truth in Lending disclosure, itemization of amount financed, statement of insurance, signature of buyer/co-buyer, owner seller, and seller assignment, DMV Notice of Sale or Transfer of a Vehicle of Vessel and odometer mileage statement, a nine page form with the vehicle description including VIN/HULL number, buyer name, seller name, bill of sale, authorization for payoff, payoff adjustment, and power of attorney, service, maintenance, repair records in the name of the defendant, stating the date of service instructions, parts and labor estimates, and customer signature for service authorization, cash receipt, IRS Forms 4789 or 8300, credit information report, record of the salesman card files, and loan approval record.

Safe Deposit Box/Private Mail Box – Business-Search Warrant

THE PREMISES known as (name of business) at (address), (city), California, (zip code), the Safe Deposit Box # (box number) in the name of (name of box holder) located at this location.

According to California Business and Professions Code 22780 a search warrant is not required to obtain information about the user or subscriber of a particular private mail box. Commercial mail receiving agencies are required to obtain Postal Service Form 1583 from each customer. The code states:

(a) A commercial mail receiving agency shall not accept a Postal Service From 1583 until positive identification has been established for the person filing the form. For purposes of this section, positive identification means any one of the following:

(1) Driver's license.

(2) State identification card.

(3) Armed forces identification card.

(4) Employment identification card which contains the bearer's signature and photograph.

(5) Any similar documentation which provides the agency with reasonable assurance of the identity of the filer.

(b) A commercial mail receiving agency shall maintain a copy of any Postal Service Form 1583 filed with the United States Postal Service. Upon the request of any law enforcement agency conducting an investigation, the commercial mail receiving agency shall make available to that law enforcement agency for purposes of that investigation and copying, its copy of the Postal Service Form 1583.

(c) A violation of this chapter is an infraction punishable by a fine of not less than one hundred dollars ($100) for the first offense, and a fine of not less than five hundred dollars ($500) for each subsequent offense.

Stock Brokerage-Search Warrant

In the name of the defendant, all stock account applications, margin account agreements, option account agreements, Federal tax forms W-9, 1099, and 4789, customer account number and record, all records and documents whether original or microfilm pertaining to receipts, canceled checks for deposits, (cash-check-securities), withdrawals, broker order tickets, buys, sells conformations, monthly statements of all stock, margin and option accounts, record of transfers and transfer authorizations, wire transmittals, precious metals transactions, application for commodity trading, monthly statements, broker order tickets, buys, sells, confirmations, money market accounts, mutual fund accounts, bond market accounts, margin calls, and Power of Attorney documents.

Title Company-Search Warrant

All actions in title and transfers from/to the defendant open or closed including real property, bulk transfers, and liquor license transfers, real estate purchase contract, receipts for deposit, take sheet, escrow guide, escrow instructions, escrow settlement sheet, copies of notary book, settlement statement, grant deed, deed of trust, preliminary title report, loan applications, insurance binders, credit reports, preliminary financial investigations report, personal notes of instruction by the escrow officer(s), loan disbursement instructions, full disclosure statement, installment loan note, amendments, changes of ownership, and riders, tax returns of applicants, copies of disbursement checks, escrow logs, and appraisal reports.

Travel Agency or Service-Search Warrant

All travel records and travel itineraries in the name of the defendant, and passengers with the defendant, Passenger Name Records (PNR), 3. agent coupons, ticketing information, itinerary denoting method of payment and fare information, such as cash, check, credit card receipts and statements, itinerary denoting method of travel, name of carrier company, carrier route/flight number, point of departure, destination, point of return, date of departure, date of return, itinerary information for direct travel, connecting travel, or tour companies, any additional history of travel booking, credit card receipts or invoices, additional reservations made for hotels or vehicle rentals, special applications, reservations, or requests for luggage, handicap assistances, dietary restrictions, pets, and/or firearms, travel insurance applications and designated beneficiary, and copies of any passports associated with the defendant.

Trust Department or Administrator-Search Warrant

Trust agreements in the name of the defendant including Powers of Attorney to act in the capacity for the defendant, fiduciary authority to act on the name of ______, trust ledgers, asset ledgers, cash ledgers, investment ledgers, stock ledgers, safekeeping ledgers, buy orders, sell orders, confirmations, income and expense ledgers, disbursement ledgers, copies of checks whether in paper, digital, or microfilm forms, wire transmittals, transfers between accounts and/or banks, drafts, stock certificates, bonds, and any item paid out of the trust.

Bank / Financial Institution Records - Bank Records-Search Warrant

Police Request

Government Code section 7480 subd. (b) provides that a police or sheriff's department or district attorney may obtain certain financial information upon request made to the financial institution when it certifies in writing that a crime report has been filed alleging certain fraudulent acts. For example, information relating to dishonored checks and overdrafts may be obtained upon certification to the financial institution, in writing, that the checks were used fraudulently. The bank will then provide a statement of account

and other records for a period of time 30 days prior to and 30 days following the alleged illegal acts. A sample written request appears at the end of this chapter.

Victimized Financial Institution

A bank may, in its discretion, lawfully turn over a customer's bank records to the police if the bank believes it is a victim of a crime committed by the customer such as a customer's use of a bank-issued credit card after having reported it stolen.

All account information in the name of (name of account holder), Social Security Number (Social Security #), (additional names or business names), Tax ID number (tax ID # if available), and any account in which (name of person) is an authorized signer thereof: in particular, such as, account number (account number(s)) in the name of (name of account holder) and account number (additional account(s) numbers, remove if not available) in the name of (additional account holder name(s)) and/or unknown other accounts for above listed account holder.

This information is to cover the period from (starting date) to (ending date) and include; all signature cards on said account(s), all monthly account statements on said account(s), microfilm copies of all items deposited to said account(s), all deposit slips to said account(s) including both sides, all deposited items to said account(s) including both sides, all checks written/paid against said account(s) including both sides, copies of application(s) for purchase of

Cashier checks, Manager's checks, Counter Checks and/or Treasurers checks and carbon copies purchased, from said account(s) and the Name of the purchaser, loan records, including applications, records of amounts borrowed, payments, collateral agreements, and ledger sheets on said account(s) and/or by account holder, all documents pertaining to loan payments made from said account(s), all miscellaneous records pertaining to the deposits or withdrawals of moneys from said account(s), any debit or credit memos on said account(s) or by Account Holder, all documents showing any bank credit agreement with, or any credit extended by, the Bank / Financial Institution to the account holder to cover overdrafts of checks drawn on said account(s), all records of "special handling" and/or "rejected items" reports and/or other records showing rejection of checks drawn against said account(s), copies of all documents pertaining to Wire Transfers / Cable Remittances / Telephone Transfers to or from said account(s), copies of all correspondence between the account holder and the Bank / Financial Institution whether sent or received, fictitious name(s) filing on said account(s), if applicable, credit card applications, monthly statements and/or records of purchases and payments by Account Holder, mortgage records and applications, copies of Promissory Notes, Records of purchase of Bearer Bonds, Safekeeping Register records, Investment and/or Custodian accounts, on said account(s) and/or by Account Holder, and safe deposit box records, including applications and records of access on said account(s) and/or by Account Holder,

Bank / Financial Institution Records - Bank Records-Affidavit

Based upon your Affiant's training, experience and conversations that your Affiant had with other Law Enforcement Officers and/or reports that your Affiant has read, your Affiant knows that Bank(s) / Financial Institute(s) maintain records that can be obtained by the use of a Search Warrant. The locations must be given the information about the accounts, persons and/or businesses that the Search Warrant is written for. The Bank(s) / Financial Institute(s) frequently maintain these records at their Corporate Offices, Central Processing and/or Data Centers. The Bank(s) / Financial Institute(s) have to supply the requested data from their own data storage centers, normally they send a copy of the Search Warrant to that location and a representative then gathers and supplies the Search Warrant ordered documents and/or data.

The Bank(s) / Financial Institute(s) cannot generally search for, gather, duplicate, and/or provide the information within ten days. Furthermore, the Bank(s) / Financial Institute(s) search, may continue their search beyond the ten-day period required for service of the Search Warrant to the extent necessary to complete the search and supply the information to the Affiant.

Bank Account Funds - Seizure of Funds at Bank-Search Warrant

IT IS HEREBY ORDERED, to seize all moneys presently in (bank branch), (address located) at (city), California, (zip code), County of (Orange), account number (account number) in the name of (name of account holder). The money may be seized by agreement and consent of an officer of the (bank branch) branch listed above; whereby the bank holds the account in suspension and does not allow any transactions relating to the account without an order from this Court. This order is issued under authority of California Penal Code Section 1524(a)(3). This Court or other assigned Court will make a determination as to distribution of these funds based upon either California Penal Code Section 1539, 1540 or the adjudication of the related felony allegation.

Bank Account Funds - Seizure of Funds at Bank-Affidavit

Based upon your Affiant's training, experience and conversations that your Affiant had with other Law Enforcement Officers and/or reports that your Affiant has read, your Affiant knows the suspect in this case has deposited and/or transferred money to the above listed Bank(s) / Financial Institute(s) and that said funds were obtained during the commission of a crime. Your Affiant requests a Court Order for the Bank(s) / Financial Institute(s) to hold the account in suspension and is to not allow transactions relating to the account without an Order from this Court. This order should be issued under authority of California Penal Code Section 1524(a)(3). This Court or other assigned Court will make a determination as to the distribution of these funds based upon either California Penal Code Section 1539, 1540 or the adjudication of the felony allegation.

The Search Warrant: Vehicles

Vehicles

Describing vehicles are no different than describing places to be searched. However, there is usually less to describe as a vehicle usually has far less in the way of descriptors than a residence or business. Common descriptors include license plates, vehicle identification numbers (VINs), or a general description of the vehicle or location if neither are known.

Vehicle - Known License Plate-Search Warrant

The use of a vehicle in the commission of a crime justifies its search. In most cases, the color, year, make, model, and license number of the vehicle to be searched are an adequate description.

THE VEHICLE described as a (year, make, model, color of vehicle) bearing California license # (veh. license number) including containers of any kind within the vehicle.

Vehicle - Known VIN (Vehicle Identification Number) -Search Warrant

THE VEHICLE described as a (year, make, model, color of vehicle) with the vehicle identification number of (VIN), including containers of any kind within the vehicle.

Vehicle - Location Known - Unknown Plate or VIN-Search Warrant

THE VEHICLE described as an approximately (year, make, model, color of vehicle) (any unique descriptor that applies to vehicle such as vehicle damage, bumper stickers, visible modifications) license number unknown, believed to be parked at or near (address), (city), California, (zip code), including containers of any kind within the vehicle.

Vehicle - Owner Known - Unknown Plate or VIN-Search Warrant

THE VEHICLE described as approximately (year, make, model, color of vehicle) (any unique descriptor that applies to vehicle) a license number unknown; believed to be owned or in the custody of (name of person), including containers of any kind within the vehicle.

Vehicle - Unknown Make or Model - Suspect Is In Control Of-Search Warrant

If you can establish that the suspect keeps or delivers contraband in whatever vehicle he happens to be using or being driving in, and that the suspect uses a number of vehicles or often uses borrowed vehicles, the warrant may then be issued for, "any vehicle under the control of or occupied by (suspect's name) at the time this warrant is served."

ANY VEHICLE in the immediate vicinity of (address), (city), California, (zip code), that is in the custody or control of (name of person) as evidence by ignition keys, or car door keys, or vehicle ownership documents in his/her possession, or on his/her person, or under his/her dominion and control, or by statements of witnesses, or any vehicle within the garages, grounds, or storage areas to be searched. Such search shall include containers of any kind within the vehicle.

Hidden Compartments-Vehicle-Search Warrant

If the vehicle has a hidden compartment or if contraband is secreted in an unusual location which may require partial disassembly of the vehicle, it is best to specifically describe the compartment or location.

THE VEHICLE described as a white 2009 Ford F150 pickup truck, California license number 1A12345, believed to be parked at or near 123 Main Street, Sacramento CA and all parts and compartments therein including the area within the truck bed. Agents are authorized to use reasonable means, including destructive or damaging measures, to recover any evidence contained therein.

Installing A GPS Tracker-Affidavit

This affidavit is submitted in support of a request for authorization for law enforcement agents to install a tracking device into a Black convertible BMW temporary paper dealer license plate from River City Auto Dealer. Identification number (VIN) XXXXXXXXXXXXXXXX located within the State of California.

Your affiant also requests authorization to monitor the tracking device for the limited purpose of tracking the vehicle's location and for gathering evidence which constitutes evidence of offenses in violation Penal Code section _______________.

The movements, location and duration of activity or inactivity of a vehicle or object under surveillance are often paramount to the solving of crime. Police surveillance and tools to aid them and document them have evolved to the point that GPS tracking devices require court authorization for installation and monitoring.

GPS tracking devices use a variety of technology depending on the make, model or manufacturer of the device. The primary objective of finding and recording a fixed location of coordinates and logging that data locally in the device itself is common. Some devices offer enhance functions or features that determine how that information is both processed and used. The GPS coordinates or similar location based technology tell the law enforcement technician where the device is or was located at a particular time on a map.

These devices require power to operate. Power may be supplied with the device when it is installed by law enforcement or the target vehicle's power can be used to supply power to the surveillance device. Certain hardware functions may notify the user when the vehicle begins to move by use of something like an accelerometer. This is useful to conserve power when the device is not in motion as well as notify law enforcement when a target vehicle or object has begun to move from a particular location. The time and location of these types of events are unpredictable and may result in information being captured while the vehicle or object is in a place like an enclosed residential garage where a person may have an expectation of privacy. Many GPS tracking device models can wirelessly transmit the recorded or real time coordinate information, or events based on other hybrid hardware and software functionality, remotely to law enforcement technicians. This monitoring allows law enforcement the ability to recover information captured by the surveillance device without making physical contact with the device and jeopardizing the existence of the investigation or destruction of evidence or equipment.

For this investigation the tracking device requires the following installation **<describe>** and will collect the following information **<describe>**

An electronic tracking device has proven to be an invaluable tool in assisting in physical surveillances in past investigations. Aided by the tracking device, the police conducting physical surveillances have been able to track the whereabouts of vehicles without having to closely follow a vehicle. The use of this tracking device reduces or eliminates the chance that the operator of the subject vehicle will detect that he is the subject of a physical surveillance while allowing law enforcement the ability to know exactly where the vehicle is located at any time. Moreover, since the individuals utilizing the above-captioned Black convertible BMW are utilizing that vehicle in furtherance of the burglaries they commit and are undoubtedly familiar with conducting surveillances themselves of the homes and surrounding area in which they commit burglaries, physical surveillance of these individuals will be extremely difficult to perform without being detected. The fact that these individuals commit burglaries during daylight hours in residential neighborhoods also makes it extremely difficult to conduct physical surveillances of them without the use of a tracking device.

In this investigation, the use of the tracking device will permit law enforcement to know exactly where the above-captioned vehicle is located, without the need for close physical surveillance of the vehicle. Close physical surveillances may result in our detection, which in turn will cause the suspects to change their plans. Furthermore, with physical surveillance there is always the possibility that the suspects will evade the surveillance teams, especially at night when such surveillances are difficult due to reduced traffic on the roads or during the daylight hours into isolated neighborhoods without raising the possibility the suspects will realize the surveillance and alter or curtail their activities.

Most importantly, in this particular case, without knowing the exact location of where this vehicle goes to, we may not be able to determine the home(s) in which they intend to burglarize or, after completing a burglary, the escape route they take to leave the area. The tracking device would allow law enforcement to determine the location, routes and destinations of the above-captioned vehicle without jeopardizing the investigation.

Investigators in placing the device may be required to make alterations or modifications to the vehicle. These modifications are required to provide power to the device and to avoid detection of the device.

Investigators may be required to re-access the vehicle during the monitoring period authorized by this order in order in order to service or remove the tracking device. Servicing may include (1) replacement of batteries; (2) replacement of device if malfunctioning; or (3) reinstallation of device if not functioning properly in its installed location.

The tracking device will also be removed prior to the end of the monitoring period authorized by this order. If the device cannot be removed, all monitoring will cease at the termination date of this order and investigators will reapply for an additional search warrant seeking the removal and recovery of the tracking device.

This warrant will only be executed surreptitiously under cover of darkness while the car is parked on a public street, public parking lot, or public parking garage, or the location described in the warrant. However, for purposes of concealment and officer safety, in order to execute this warrant at night it may require the warrant be served during the hours of 10:00 p.m. and 7:00 a.m. Therefore, I am requesting the warrant be authorized for nighttime service pursuant to Penal Code section 1533.

I am also requesting exception from the normal knock and notice requirement of Penal Code section 1531. Knock and notice is required to alert occupants of premises to the presence and imminent entry of law enforcement. The purpose of knock and notice has two reasons: privacy and safety; to avoid interrupting the private and personal functions of the occupants in their premises and to protect both the occupants and police from the use of deadly force in the event the occupants believed their premises were being invaded by robbers or other attackers as opposed to the authorized entry of police. Neither privacy nor safety is at issue here. Once again, only a vehicle, which the U.S. Supreme Court has recognized as having a lesser expectation of privacy than a residence, will be entered here. And, as any entry will take place at night in a public place when no one is around, safety is not of the same concern as it would be for a residence

Additionally, I request officers executing this warrant be excused from the immediate receipt requirement of Penal Code section 1535. Obviously, notifying the vehicle's owner or custodian that a warrant was executed to install a tracking device in the vehicle will alert the owner/custodian to law enforcement's ongoing investigation and prompt the person to locate and remove the tracking device or to move or destroy any contraband from related premises before a subsequent warrant can be obtained and executed. This request is further supported by the fact officers will not remove any property, other than electrical current, from the vehicle further negating the necessity of leaving a receipt and inventory form. However, because I am aware the owner of the vehicle is entitled to same, at the end of the investigation, I will provide notice to the owner that a tracking device was attached to his/her vehicle during the stated period of time.

Since the subjects of this investigation have committed the known burglaries during the daylight hours and may conduct surveillances of residences to be targeted at nighttime hours and dispose of the stolen property at any time of the day or night, I am requesting that this Court authorize monitoring of the requested tracking device 24 hours per day, seven days a week, for a period of 45 days from the date of the Order requested herein, and that such authorization may be extended for an additional 45-day periods upon further application to this Court.

I am further requesting that a return of the Order requested herein be made before this Court without unnecessary delay following the expiration of the 45-day period, unless said 45-day is extended by further Order of this Court. Moreover, I am respectfully requesting that such return take the form of a printout (or contained on a CD) of the GPS device data or any other manner prescribed by this Court, and that said return shall remain under the seal of this Court until further Order of this Court.

In light of the nature of this application, your affiant requests an order sealing both the application and warrant. This request is made to implement the privilege under Evidence Code sections 1040 to 1042 pursuant to the California Supreme Court decision in *People v. Hobbs* (1994) 7 C4th 948.

Your affiant believes that the information contained in both the application and warrant would serve to will alert the owner/custodian to law enforcement's ongoing investigation and prompt the person to locate and remove the tracking device or to move or destroy any contraband from related premises before a subsequent warrant can be obtained and executed. Consequently, your affiant requests both the application and warrant be sealed pending any further orders of the court.

WHEREFORE, your affiant respectively requests that the Court authorize searching officers or their authorized representatives, including, but not limited to, other law enforcement agents and technicians assisting in the above-described investigation, to enter and install within 10 days a mobile tracking device in or on the subject vehicle; to monitor the signals from that tracking device, for a period of 45 days pursuant to the Court's order, including signals produced from inside private garages and other locations not open to the public or visual surveillance, and signals produced in the event that the subject vehicle leaves the California but remains within the United States pursuant to 18 U.S.C. § 3117; and to delay provision of notice of the search warrant .

The Search Warrant: People

People

Similar to locations and vehicles, people can be specified in the search warrant as areas to be searched for evidence and contraband. A person should be described with as much reasonable particularity as possible.

Person – Known-Search Warrant

The description of a person should include the name, sex, race, age, height, weight, hair color, eye color, and distinguishing marks to the extent they are known. Again, as with a vehicle, if only the person is to be searched or if the description is incomplete or uncertain, then his or her probable location should be given.

THE PERSON known as (name of person), described as a (male/female) (descent), approximately (age) years of age, approximately (feet) ft (inches) inches tall, weighing approximately (weight) pounds, with (hair color) hair, (eye color) eyes, born on (DOB), with California drivers license #: (CDL).

Person - Known by Nickname- Residing At Location-Affidavit

If the search of the person is being conducted in conjunction with the search of his location or residence, he may be described as being at that location.

THE PERSON known as (nickname used), described as a (male/female) (descent), approximately (age) years of age, approximately (feet) ft (inches) inches tall, approximately (weight) pounds, with (hair color) hair, (eye color) eyes, with (any scars, tattoos, etc.), believed to be visiting, or residing at (address), (city), California (zip code).

For example:

. . . THE PERSON of "Rich," a white male adult, approximately 70 years old, 5'11", 200 lbs., brown hair and eyes, tip of middle finger on right hand missing, and believed to be within the above described premises.

Person - Unknown - At Location-Affidavit

THE PERSON described as a (male/female) (descent), approximately (age) years of age, approximately (feet) ft (inches) inches tall, approximately (weight) pounds, with (hair color) hair, (eye color) eyes, with (any scars, tattoos, etc.), believed to be visiting, or residing at (address), (city), California (zip code).

Person – Police Impersonator -Affidavit

Based upon my training and experience:

I am aware subjects who impersonate Peace Officers; purchase, manufacture, and otherwise obtain items such as uniforms, altered clothing, police duty equipment, handguns/firearms, business cards, and credentials/identification cards which lead a reasonable person to believe that a the subject wearing the garb of a Peace Officer was in fact a member of the law enforcement community.

I am aware those who impersonate Peace Officers will often equip their vehicles with radios, light bars, sirens, prisoner transport cages, and other standard issue police vehicle equipment. I believe evidence of the same will be obtained from searching the 2012 Ford F250 truck California license plate ________ registered to __________.

I am aware those who impersonate Peace Officers will frequently obtain the items used in the impersonation from internet and online marketers. I am aware these transactions generate items such as bills of sale, invoices, and packaging materials used to ship the merchandise.

Person – Police Impersonator –Search Warrant

Any firearms, including rifles and handguns

Receipts for the purchase and ownership of arms and ammunition.

Military Police/Federal Police Officer/Peace Officer related equipment, including by way of example and not by way of limitation; ballistic kevlar helmets, military load bearing equipment, uniforms, duty equipment (belt, holster, magazine pouches, baton and holster, government issued radios and holders, handcuffs and holder.

Items of indicia which tend to show the identity or the person or persons in control of the premises located at _______ including by way of example and not by way of limitation: utility bills; rent receipts; canceled mail envelopes and cards; telephone bills; canceled checks; bank statements; savings account passbooks; deposit receipts; passports; diaries; social security cards; drivers licenses; vehicle registration and title papers; land titles; escrow papers; tax receipts; identification cards; photographs and keys.

Paper writings or records that show evidence impersonating a Peace Officer, manufacturing government credentials or identification; including by way of example, and not by way of limitation: address books, ledgers, lists, notebooks, computer systems, computer disks, and audio and video recordings.

Proceeds, goods, or items of value gained by impersonating a peace officer; including by way of example and not by way of limitation: Military or Law Enforcement equipment, membership to Military of Law Enforcement association (such as the California Narcotics Officer Association, National Tactical Officers Association, Unites States Police Canine Association, Military Police Association, and etc.)

Cellular telephones and pagers.

Records of the purchase or acquisition of military and or law enforcement supplies such as receipts, packing slips, invoices, shipping envelops, and boxes

The Search Warrant: Computers and Internet Service Providers

Computers

Computers play an important role in multiple different types of criminal investigations. Due to the storage capacity of modern computers and the variety of information contain inside those computers, specific language describing the types of evidence to be searched for has evolved. Recover of the evidence contained in computers has spawned the formation of high technology crime task forces who specialize in the recovery of different types of computer data. Consult a forensic specialist before executing a search warrant for computer related evidence and there are specialized considerations which should be addressed in the affidavit, the search warrant, and the manner the evidence is collected.

Computer(s) - Seizure and Search-Search Warrant

All electronic data processing and storage devices, computers and computer systems, such as central processing units, internal and peripheral storage devices such as fixed disks, internal and external hard drives, floppy disk drives and diskettes, tape drives and tapes, optical storage devices, dongles, encryption keys, personal data assistants (PDA's) or other memory storage devices; and any/all peripheral input/output devices such as keyboards, printers, video display monitors, optical readers and related communication devices such as modems, associated telephone sets, speed dialers, and/or other controlling devices, plotters, software to run programs, connecting cables and plugs, peripherals such as joysticks, mouse, or other input devices, scanners, writing pads, manuals, connecting switches, telephones and telephone cables, and interface devices; system documentation, operating logs and documentation, software and instructional manuals. Computing or data processing software, stored on any type of medium such as: hard disks, floppy disks, CD-R's, CD-RW's, DVD's, cassette tapes, or other permanent or transient storage medium.

Any records, whether stored on paper, on magnetic media such as tape, cassette, disk, diskette or on memory storage devices such as optical disks, programmable instruments such as telephones, "electronic calendar\address books" calculators, or any other storage media, together with indicia of use, ownership, possession, or control of such records.

Any written or computer communication in printed or stored medium such as E-Mail and Chat Logs whether in active files, deleted files or unallocated space on the hard drive, floppy drive or any data storage media.

Search of all of the above items is for files, data, images, software, operating systems, deleted files, altered files, system configurations, drive and disk configurations, date and time, and unallocated and slack space, for evidence.

With respect to computer systems and any items listed above found during the execution with this Search Warrant, the searching Peace Officers are authorized to seize and book said computer systems and any items listed above and transfer them to a Law Enforcement Agency location prior to commencing the search of the items. Furthermore, said search may continue beyond the ten-day period beginning upon issuance of this Search Warrant, to the extent necessary to complete the search on the computer systems and any items listed above.

Computer(s) - Seizure and Search-Affidavit

Based upon your Affiant's training, experience and conversations that your Affiant had with other Law Enforcement Officers and/or reports that your Affiant has read, your Affiant knows that computer and computer systems commonly consist of electronic data processing and storage devices, with central processing units, internal and peripheral storage devices such as fixed disks, external hard disks, floppy disk drives and diskettes, tape drives and tapes, optical storage devices, dongles or encryption keys, personal data assistants (PDA's) or other memory storage devices. They also consist of peripheral input/output devices such as keyboards, printers, video display monitors, optical readers and related communication devices such as modems, associated telephone sets, speed dialers, or other controlling devices, plotters, software to run programs, connecting cables and plugs, peripherals such as joysticks, mouse, or other input devices, scanners, writing pads, manuals, connecting switches, telephones and telephone cables, and interface devices. There is system documentation, operating logs and documentation, software and instructional manuals for the computers and computer systems. Computing or data processing software, stored on any type of medium such as: hard disks, floppy disks, CD-R's, CD-RW's, DVD's, cassette tapes, or other permanent or transient storage medium and other forms of magnetic media containing computer information.

Your Affiant requests any records, whether stored on paper, on magnetic media such as tape, cassette, disk, diskette or on memory storage devices such as optical disks, programmable instruments such as telephones, "electronic calendar\address books" calculators, or any other storage media, together with indicia of use, ownership, possession, or control of such records.

Your Affiant requests any written or computer communication in printed or stored medium such as E-Mail and Chat Logs whether in active files, deleted files or unallocated space on the hard drive, floppy drive or any data storage media.

It is your Affiant's experience that computer system searches and examinations cannot be completed within ten days in which the Search Warrant must be served and the Return to Search Warrant filed. This is due in part because the Police Agency, that completes the computer search and examinations, it is common for them to have multiple cases working at the same time and it can take several weeks to complete. It is requested that the Search Warrant and Return to Search Warrant be filed and that the computer search, examinations, and investigation be allowed to continue.

Computer – Search-Search Warrant

Investigating officers are authorized, at their discretion, to seize all "computer systems," "computer programs or software," and "supporting documentation" as defined by Penal Code section 502, subd. (b), including any supporting hardware, software or documentation that is necessary to the use of the system or is necessary to recover digital evidence from the system and any associated peripherals that are believed to contain some or all of the evidence described in the warrant, and to conduct an off-site search of the seized items for the evidence described. Investigating officers and those agents acting under the direction of the investigating officers are authorized to access all computer data to determine if the data contains "property," "records," and "information" as described above. If necessary, investigating officers are authorized to employ the use of outside experts, acting under the direction of the investigating officers, to access and preserve computer data. The investigating officer has [insert current forensic turnaround time + 10 days] days from the date of seizure to determine if the seized computer systems and associated peripherals contain some or all of the evidence described in the warrant. If no evidence of criminal activity is discovered relating to the seized computer systems and associated peripherals, the system will be returned promptly.

Computer – Search-Affidavit

Based upon your Affiant's training, experience and conversations that your Affiant had with other Law Enforcement Officers and/or reports that your Affiant has read, your Affiant requests the search of computers and computer system components such as; central processing units (CPU), internal and peripheral storage devices such as internal or external hard drives, removable storage devices and disks/hard drives, floppy disk drives and diskettes, CD-R, CD-RW, DVD drives and disks, tape drives and tapes, optical storage devices or other memory storage devices, integral RAM or ROM devices; peripheral input/output devices such as keyboards, mouse, touch pads, printers, scanners, plotters, cameras, video display monitors, modems, external data storage devices, optical readers and related communication devices such as acoustic or electrical modems, or other controlling devices such as diskettes, CD-R, CD-RW, DVD disks, power back-up devices, connecting switches, interface devices, software to run programs, connecting cables, switches, power sources, and plugs.

Search of all of the above components is for files, data, images, software, operating systems, deleted files, system configurations, drive and disk configurations, date and time, unallocated and slack space, for evidence.

With respect to computer systems and any items listed above, the Peace Officers are authorized to search the booked evidence. It is your Affiant's experience that computer system searches and examinations cannot be completed within ten days, in which the Search Warrant must be served and the Return to Search Warrant filed. This is due in part because the Police Agency, that completes the computer search and examinations, has multiple computer cases working at the same time and it can take several weeks to complete. It is requested that the ten-day requirement be waived to provide your Affiant ample time to process and comply with the Search Warrant in a timely manner. The Return to Search Warrant will be filed promptly upon completion of the computer search and examinations that are filed with the Case Investigator.

ISP - Information Request - Internet Service Provider-Search Warrant

Searching for information from an Internet Service Provider (ISP) such as Google, Facebook, eBay, PayPal, and Craigslist can yield a tremendous amount of information relevant to a variety of criminal investigations. There are a number of specific factors to bear in mind when working with ISPs.

First, many of the larger ISPs have created law enforcement guides answering common questions and outlining their data retention policies and procedures. The guides are invaluable when writing a search warrant for information from an ISP.

Second, there are varying degrees of cooperation from some ISPs. An important rule to remember is that is you do not specify the evidence or information to be retrieved from an ISP; they are not required to offer it.

Third, ISPs will notify the customer/subscriber unless they are directed otherwise. Make sure you include non-disclosure language in your search warrants for ISPs.

Fourth, some ISPs view law enforcement search warrants and other legal demands such as court orders and subpoenas and court orders as 'requests.' Unfortunately, these ISPs act as if they are doing law enforcement a favor by responding to the warrant and fail to understand that a search warrant is an order from the court.

Suggested search warrant language for obtaining information from an ISP includes:

All (Internet Service Provider) stored electronic communications, including Email, digital images, buddy list(s), and any other files associated with User and/or User account(s) identified as:

(Users Name, Address)

(Email Address)

All connections logs and records of User activity for each such account including:

Connection dates and times, disconnection dates and times, method of connection, for example, data transfer volume, user name associated with the connections, telephone caller identification records, any other connection information, such as the Internet Protocol address of the source of the connection.

Connection information for the other computer to which the user of the above-referenced accounts connected, by any means, during the connection period, including the destination IP address, connection date and time, disconnect date and time, method of connection to the destination computer, and all other information related to the connection of this ISP provider.

Any other records related to the above referenced Names and User Names, such as, correspondence, billing records, records of contact by any person or entity regarding the above referenced Name(s) and User Name(s), and any other subscriber information, referenced Name, and any other Subscriber information, Subscriber's address(es), contact person(s), account information, order form(s), account opened date(s), Screen Name(s) / Email address log(s), dial-up log(s), read mail, unread mail, sent mail, other screen names / Email address(es) assigned to the account, credit card / payment information and any identifying information which would tend to Identify the person(s) subscribing for service, such as dates of birth, social security numbers, credit card number(s), home and/or business address(es), and home and business telephone numbers.

Documentation of any complaints made against the subscriber for inappropriate conduct while using (Internet Service Provider), if available.

ISP - Information Request - Internet Service Provider-Affidavit

Based upon your Affiant's training, experience and conversations that your Affiant had with other Law Enforcement Officers and/or reports that your Affiant has read, your Affiant knows that Internet Service Providers (ISP) typically maintains records that are relevant to this investigation. Subscriber and billing records can establish common and control over the computer and premises where the computer is found, also Emails involved in this investigation. The substance of Emails demonstrates the relationships of parties and the state of mind of the sender. The records that are needed from the ISP providers are Dates and Times of connections and disconnections, User Names, types of connections, other records relating to Names and Users Names, and stored electronic communications. Your Affiant also relies that the ISP sometimes get complaints about the ISP Users and these can assist in the investigation.

Internet Service Provider - Google

Investigators should confirm the appropriate business entity name, method of service, custodian of records' name, addresses, and telephone numbers before drafting the search warrant. Many internet service providers have law enforcement guides which detail what kind of information they store and can access. Internet service providers can be researched at http://www.search.org/programs/hightech/isp/

THE PREMISES known as Google, Inc. Legal Investigations Support, 1600 Amphitheatre Parkway Mountain View, CA 94043 phone: 650-253-3425 Fax Number: 650-249-3429 E-mail Address: uslawenforcement@google.com.

NOTE: Google services include: Search, GMail, Talk, YouTube, Blogger, AdWords, AdSense, Checkout, Orkut, Picasa, Sites, Groups, Docs, Maps, Earth, Video, and Android among others.

Facebook

Facebook has become the number one social networking site which inevitably invites a variety of criminals to it. Facebook has instituted several specific policies for law enforcement to follow in order to retrieve evidence from their site.

Facebook will only respond to three different types of requests:

1)   Preservation letters submitted pursuant to 18 USC 2703(f) which directs Facebook to preserve existing account information for 90 days pending service of formal legal process.

2)   Formal legal requests such as court order issued pursuant to 18 USC 2703(d), search warrants, and subpoenas.   Facebook's response time varies depending on the complexity of the case and the volume of records requested.

3)   Exigent circumstances requests using Facebook's Emergency Request Form.   Exigent circumstances are typically defined as an imminent threat to life or serious bodily harm.   Facebook evaluates these requests and will only respond if they have a good faith belief that standard has been met.

Important Considerations When Submitting Search Warrants to Facebook

Facebook will automatically disable accounts which provided false or misleading information in the profile or try to circumvent their privacy measures. Likewise, Facebook will disable accounts engaged in illegal activity, even if that activity is brought to their attention through a law enforcement search warrant. If Facebook shutting down your suspect's account you must clearly specify "**DO NOT DISABLE UNTIL XX/XX/XXXX**" on your request. However, if the suspect's account has already been reported to Facebook's operations team, independent of the subpoena compliance group, they may disable the account.

Facebook will only return information data which is no older than 90 days from the date of receipt of a search warrant. If you require older information you must specify a greater date range.

Facebook requires search warrants submitted to them include the law enforcement agency name, the peace officers name and shield/badge/or identification number, an authorized email address to respond to, a phone number, including extension to direct any questions to, the department's mailing address, and a response date.

Facebook asks for two to six weeks to process the information demanded in a search warrant. This does not always correspond with the ten day service/response requirements in most search warrants. Depending on the urgency of the investigation, you may choose to demand the records within the time frame specific in the search warrant, or include a time extension in the warrant allowing them additional time to respond.

Facebook identifies accounts by email address, user identification, or user name. If you have identified a suspect's profile page, their Facebook ID is contained in the Uniform Resource Locator (URL) found in the search bar of your internet browser. For example www.facebook.com/profile.php?id=12345678 contains the ID 12345678 which is used to identify their user. Facebook follows a similar pattern for Group Identification and User Names. Group Identification numbers are specified as 'gid' as in www.facebook.com/group.php?gid=1234567890 and user names appear pretty obvious such as www.facebook.com/john.doe. Facebook requests the date the information was obtained to assist them with locating the appropriate records.

What type of legal process was used will determine the type of data which will be returned. Facebook maintains Basic Subscriber Information, sometimes referred to as Neoselect, which may include the following data:

The user's identification number, the user's email address, the date and time the account was created (NOTE: This will be in Coordinated Universal Time and often requires the use of a converter in order to view the appropriate date and time in your geographic region/time zone.), the last two to three days of logins prior to the request (again in Coordinated Universal Time), and the subscriber's registered phone number.

Facebook can also provide Expanded Subscriber Content, sometimes referred to as a Neoprint. This information may include the subscriber's profile contact information, mini-feeds, the user's status update history, any 'shares' with other Facebook users, notes, wall postings, friends listing (which include the friend's Facebook ID, group listing (with Facebook Group ID, future and past events, and video listings with filenames.

You may also be able to obtain user photos, sometimes referred to as a User Photoprint, which may include photos uploaded by the user and photos uploaded by other users that have the user tagged in them.

Facebook can also provide group information and the basic subscriber information of the group administrator/.creator and group status.

Pursuant to a search warrant, Facebook can provide information regarding private messages if the information was retained.

Internet Protocol (IP) address information is, as described by Facebook, "very limited and frequently incomplete." The data includes the data and time the account was accessed (in Pacific Standard Time as opposed to the Coordinated Universal Time format the other data is returned in), the Facebook ID account accessed, and the IP address used to access the account (NOTE: This will frequently require an additional search warrant to another ISP.)

Search warrants for Facebook should be addressed to, and may be served at:

Facebook, Inc.
Security Department/Custodian of Records
1601 California Avenue
Palo Alto, CA 94304
Fax 650-644-3229
Email: subpoena@facebook.com

Ebay/PayPal

eBay and PayPal are able to search based on the specific email address of a suspect, their full name, and any associated aliases, any known addresses or phone numbers, credit card and/or bank account numbers, and known Auction Identification numbers, and/or item numbers.

eBay will provide the following information upon receipt of a search warrant: the full registration of the target, include the billing and mailing addresses, the Internet Protocol (IP) address (at the time the account was establish only), the complete sales and bid history of the target (NOTE: bidder information will only be provided when specifically requested), credit card and checking account information, and any fraud complaints. Additionally, they can provide auction, fixed price, and eBay store records. Most account records are maintained indefinitely while most transactions records are maintained for two years. Unfortunately, records may not be available for inactive or closed accounts.

PayPal will provide: all account information including, names, addresses, phone numbers, email addresses, Social Security Numbers (if available), any associated financial accounts, records of complaints, and records of completed transactions. PayPal retains all accounts indefinitely.

You must specify whether you are requesting eBay records, PayPal records, or both. You must also specify if you want the accounts left open.

An important point to note is that in order to obtain all subject operated accounts, you must include "any and all related accounts" in the search warrant. Also note that records are returned in Pacific Standard Time.

Unfortunately, eBay does not store photos, images, or full item descriptions, and is unable to provide those records.

Similar to other ISPs, you must have a non-disclosure order included in your search warrant to prevent eBay/PayPal from notifying their customer.

Be sure to include the email address, phone number, fax number, and physical address of the affiant's agency so they can properly return the records and/or contact you if there are any questions or problems.

EBay and PayPal may be contacted at:

Fraud Investigations Team

2211 North First Street

San Jose, CA 95131

408-967-9915 (fax)

408-967-9916 (automated message system only)

ISP - Non-Disclosure Order – Internet Service Provider-Search Warrant

Pursuant to an official criminal investigation of a suspected felony being conducted by River City Police Department, IT IS HEREBY ORDERED that (ISP - Internet Service Provider) furnish, upon presentation of this Search Warrant, all records described in this Search Warrant. There is probable cause to believe that disclosure of this Search Warrant or the criminal investigation could impede the investigation being conducted. IT IS HEREBY ORDERED that (ISP - Internet Service Provider) refrain from directly or indirectly disclosing the existence of this Search Warrant or the criminal investigation to the Targeted Accounts or any person associated therewith until further notice of this court or another court of competent jurisdiction. IT IS HEREBY ORDERED that if for any reason (ISP - Internet Service Provider) alters the service associated with the Targeted Accounts or any person associated therewith, (ISP - Internet Service Provider) shall not reveal that it has received legal process or that the alteration of service is related to receipt of legal process.

ISP - Non-Disclosure Order – Internet Service Provider-Affidavit

Based upon your Affiant's training, experience and conversations that your Affiant had with other Law Enforcement Officers and/or reports that your Affiant has read, your Affiant requests that the (ISP - Internet Service Provider) furnish all records described in this Search Warrant. There is probable cause to believe that disclosure of this Search Warrant or the criminal investigation could impede the investigation being conducted. Your Affiant needs the (ISP - Internet Service Provider) to refrain from directly or indirectly disclosing the existence of this Search Warrant or the criminal investigation to the Targeted Accounts or any person associated therewith. Your Affiant requests a Court Order be issued for Non-Disclosure by the (ISP - Internet Service Provider) about this Search Warrant or the criminal investigation.

The Search Warrant: Child Pornography

Child Pornography-Search Warrant

. . . . photographs, slides, photographic negatives, computers and the files contained therein, drawings and other pictorial representations of a [age, sex, race] child either nude or dressed; photographs, slides, photographic negatives, drawings, and other pictorial representations of other children, nude or dressed; undeveloped film, exposed or unexposed; writings relating to sexual activity with children including notebooks, diaries, logs and correspondence; video and audio tape; receipts for the developing of photographic film; cameras and related photographic equipment; videotape games and records; audiotape records; and articles of personal property tending to establish the identity of the persons in control of the premises, vehicles, storage areas, and containers being searched including computers and the electronic files contained within, utility company receipts, rent receipts, addressed envelopes and keys.

Child Pornography-Affidavit

Based on my training, experience, and discussions with other law enforcement officers, I have learned that there are many types of preferential sex offenders. Some of these offenders have a primary sexual interest in children and are often referred to as pedophiles. These persons receive sexual gratification from actual contact with children and/or from fantasy involving children, through the use of photographs and/or digital images that can be stored on computer storage media. This affidavit deals with these types of offenders.

These offenders often collect sexually explicit material consisting of pictures, films, videotapes, magazines, negatives, photographs, correspondence, mailing lists, books and slides. They may use these materials for their own sexual gratification and fantasy and/or to show children in an attempt to lower the child's inhibitions. The collection may be culled and refined over time, but the size of the collection tends to increase. Such persons rarely, if ever, dispose of their sexually explicit materials, especially when they have taken the photographs or made the videos involved, as these materials are treated as prized possessions.

Collectors of child pornography almost always maintain and possess their material in the privacy and security of their homes or some other secure location where it is readily available. The collector is aroused while viewing the collection and, acting on that arousal, he often masturbates thereby fueling and reinforcing his attraction to children. This is most easily accomplished in the privacy of his own home.

Collectors of sexually explicit images of minors often times seek to correspond and meet with one another to share information and material in an effort to increase the size of or enhance their collections. Typically, it is not until these collections are uncovered by law enforcement or others that the collectors destroy or seek alternatives and secure hiding places to store their collection.

Collectors of child pornography often collect, read, copy, or maintain names, addresses, phone numbers or lists of persons who have similar sexual interests. They may have been collected by personal contact or through advertisements in various publications. These contacts are maintained as a means of personal referral, exchange, and commercial profit. These names may be maintained electronically, in the original publication, in phone or notebooks, or merely on scraps of paper. These persons also often correspond or meet with one another to share information and identities of their victims as a means of gaining status, trust, acceptance and psychological support.

The Internet has provided preferential sex offenders and collectors of child pornography with a virtually anonymous venue in which they can meet other people with the same or similar sexual interests and electronically exchange pictures of children or of adults engaged in sexual activity with children. These images are readily and easily available on the Internet. These images can then be downloaded and stored on the computer or other computer storage media and then viewed on the computer monitor at any time. These digital images can be attached to e-mail messages, transferred over the internet, and stored in an individual's e-mail account. These persons may also participate in chat rooms in order to communicate with other like-minded individuals and thereby legitimize their conduct and beliefs.

Preferential sex offenders will often maintain names, addresses, phone numbers, of victims, victim's friends, or victims of other child molesters, athletic rosters and school rosters in the same manner as described above. These persons often collect and maintain photographs of children they are or with whom they have been involved. These photos may depict children fully clothed, in various stages of undressing, totally nude, or involved in various activities not necessarily sexually explicit in nature.

It is not uncommon for these offenders to maintain diaries relating to sexual encounters with children. These accounts of their sexual experiences are used as a means of reliving the encounter. Such diaries might consist of notebooks, scraps of paper, formal diaries or computer entries in a home computer.

Child Pornography - Computers / Storage Media Used-Affidavit

Based upon your Affiant's training, experience and conversations that your Affiant had with other Law Enforcement Officers and/or reports that your Affiant has read, your Affiant knows that child pornographers generally prefer to store images of child pornography in electronic format as computer files. The computer's ability to store images in digital format makes a computer an ideal repository for child pornography. Portable disk(s) can contain hundreds (100's) or thousands (1,000's) of child pornography images. A computer hard drive can contain thousands of child pornography images in very high resolution. The images can easily be sent or received from computer users over the Internet. Child pornography files and disks that contain the files can be mislabeled or hidden to evade detection.

Child Pornography - Computers Used To Produce-Affidavit

Based upon your Affiant's training, experience and conversations that your Affiant had with other Law Enforcement Officers and/or reports that your Affiant has read, your Affiant knows that it is common for Child Pornographers to use computers to produce both still and moving images of child pornography. A Suspect that creates Child Pornography can use a digital camera to take photographs or videos then load them directly onto computers. The output from the camera can be stored, transferred and/or printed directly from the computer. Producers of Child Pornography can use devises known as scanners to transfer photographs into computers in readable formats. All of these devices, as well as computers, used with Child Pornography contain evidence of the violations of the crime

Child Pornography - Internet Service Provider (ISP)-Affidavit

Based upon your Affiant's training, experience and conversations that your Affiant had with other Law Enforcement Officers and/or reports that your Affiant has read, your Affiant knows that (Internet Service Provider (ISP)) is an Email server provider. The suspect can receive and/or distribute child pornography digital images over the Internet by the use of the Email server. The suspect's computer and/or media may not have the Child Pornography digital images; they may only be on the Internet Service Provider's server. In order to possibly identify any other suspects who have traded, given and/or sold Child Pornography with (Screen Name, Email Address or other Identifiers) and/or any victims who have been victimized by these individuals with Child Pornography, your Affiant needs all available information that (Internet Service Provider (ISP)) may have in their custody including copies of Email(s) and attachments, subscriber information and billing information.

The Search Warrant: Telephones, Cell Phones, Records, and Wiretaps

Telephone Records (Basic)-Search Warrant

Out-of-State Telephone Companies

California Penal Code section 1524.2 allows law enforcement officers to obtain telephone records that are in the possession of a foreign corporation that provides electronic communication to the general public. This section provides for the issuance of search warrants "for records that are in the actual or constructive possession of a foreign corporation that provides electronic communication service . . . to the general public . . ." This section further provides that the corporation shall have five business days to produce the records.

California Corporations Code section 2105 now requires that all foreign corporations doing business in California file a statement with the California Secretary of State listing the name of an agent within the state upon whom search warrants issued pursuant to Penal Code section 1524.2 can be served even though the actual records are located out of state. The name and address of such agent can be obtained by visiting the Secretary of State's business web portal at http://kepler.sos.ca.gov/.

SUBSCRIBER, BILLING, CREDIT, TOLL RECORDS, TEXT MESSAGES (including content) and CALL DETAIL INFORMATION (CELL SITE and ADDRESS LOCATIONS and GPS location information if enabled) for the monthly billing periods that covers September 1, 2011 through November 9, 2011 through thirty days after this court order is issued for the telephone number listed below. Please deliver the requested data in an "Excel" or delimited "CSV" (non-pdf) format preferably via E-Mail to [INSERT EMAIL]

ADDITIONAL ORDERS: It is also ordered as follows:

GPS Locations: Metro PCS is directed to provide real time cell tower information on request, as well as, to query the location of the phone if it is enabled with a Global Positioning System (GPS) interface.

Release of Information: MetroPCS, Inc. shall furnish affiant with all information gathered pursuant to this order in a reasonable time (five business days) while this order is in effect.

Non-disclosure: Having determined that there is probable cause to believe that the disclosure of the existence or execution of this order would impede a criminal investigation, it is ordered that MetroPCS, Inc., its officers, employees and agents not disclose to any person any information regarding the existence or execution of this order, or any information obtained pursuant to this order, unless ordered to do so by this Court, as such disclosure would impede the investigation.

JURISDICTION: This court has jurisdiction to issue this order pursuant to 18 USCS ss 3121 *et seq*, California Penal Code ss 1523 *et seq*, California Code of Civil Procedure ss 128, 187 and United States v. New York Telephone company (1977) 434 US 159.

Telephone Records (Expanded)-Search Warrant

Subscriber information

This should give you the name, address, phone numbers, and other personal identifying information relating to the subscriber.

Account comments

Anytime the provider has contact with the customer or modifies the customer's account a notation will be made by a service representative on the account.

Credit information

Many providers run a credit report on customer prior to activating the account

Billing records

Do not ask for toll information; that is a landline term for long distance. Specify the time period desired. Billing records are intended for the customer and typically appear different from other call detail records as they do not show information such as cell towers.

Outbound and inbound call detail

This is the real time, current activity that is not yet on the customer's bill and includes information they might not normally see such as cell tower information.

Call origination / termination location

For some carriers this information may only be available for a limited time (45 days) and gives location information on cell sites used, length of call, date, time, and numbers dialed.

Physical address of cell sites and RF coverage map

Needed to determine where cell site is located when you receive inbound & outbound or call origination & termination location. The RF coverage map models the theoretical radio frequency coverage of the towers in the system. You will want to limit this request to a specified geographical area. Most providers do not routinely send this with their response so you may need to re-contact them to obtain it.

Any other cellular telephone numbers that dial the same numbers as (xxx) xxx-xxxx

Note: If you want to know who calls the same number the target calls (for example a pager or landline number). Depending on the provider this information may only be available for a limited time.

Subscriber information on any cellular numbers that (xxx) xxx-xxxx dials

Subscriber information on the carrier's network that is dialing the target.

All of the above records whether possessed by cellular service provider [target of warrant] or any other cellular service provider

If you anticipate the suspect may be roaming or if the number is roaming in the providers market, you may be able to obtain information from other cellular carriers if you include this language in your description of records.

All stored communications or files, including voice mail, email, digital images, buddy lists, and any other files associated with user accounts identified as: account(s) xxxxxx, mobile numbers (xxx) xxx-xxxx, or e-mail account bigdog123@gmail.com.

Cellular service providers now offer similar services to an internet service provider (ISP) and maintain the same type of records such as text messaging, e-mail, and file storage for the transfer of data including digital pictures. In order to access stored voicemail messages the provider may have to reset the user's password which might alert them to the investigation.

L. All connection logs and records of user activity for each such account including:

      1. Connection dates and times.

      2. Disconnect dates and times.

      3. Method of connection (e.g., telnet, ftp, http)

      4. Data transfer volume.

      5. User name associated with the connections.

6. Telephone caller identification records.

> 7. Any other connection information, such as the Internet Protocol (IP) address of the device source of the connection. information related to the connection from cellular service provider.

Note: The above is a standard request made to ISP to track connection information. Remember with the type of cellular service offered today the user can send a message from the phone or from the associated account via a computer or other access device.

Any other records or accounts, including archived records related or associated to the above referenced names, user names, or accounts and any data field name definitions that describe these records.

Note: This is the catch all to use when you want everything. This request also includes "archived" information. Many companies now "archive" records thus allowing for the preservation of subscriber records for a significant time. Archived records are usually stored in a spread sheet format encompassing a variety of data fields. You *must request the data field name definitions in order to understand the spreadsheet.*

N.) PUK for SIM card # __________

Note: Subscriber Identity Module (SIM) is a smart card inside of a GSM cellular phone that encrypts voice and data transmissions and stores data about the specific user so that the user can be identified and authenticated to the network supplying the service. The SIM also stores data such as personal phone settings specific to the user and phone numbers. SIM cards can be password protected by the user. Even with this protection SIM cards may still be unlocked with a personal unlock key (PUK) that is available from the service provider. Note that after ten wrong PUK codes, the SIM card locks forever.

Telephone Records-Affidavit (General)

Through experience and training, your affiant knows cellular service providers maintain records related to subscriber information, account registration, credit information, billing and airtime records, outbound and inbound call detail, connection time and dates, Internet routing information (Internet Protocol number), and message content, that may assist in the identification or last known locations of person/s accessing and utilizing the account.

Through experience and training, your affiant knows that the cellular service provider maintains records that include cell site information and GPS location. Cell site information shows which cell site a particular cellular telephone was within at the time of the cellular phone's usage. Some model cellular phones are GPS enabled which allows the provider and user to determine the exact geographic position of the phone. Further, the cellular service provider maintains cell cite maps that show the geographical location of all cell sites within its service area. Using the cell site geographical location or GPS information, officers would be able to determine the physical location of the individuals using the listed cell phone numbers.

Telephone Records-Affidavit (Robbery)

Based upon my training and experience I know it is common for subjects to mask or hide their identity through multiple cellular and telephone accounts in order to conceal the identity of co-conspirators directly or indirectly involved in criminal activity. It is also common for witnesses, victims' and/or suspects of violent crimes such as a robbery to receive or make calls to other witnesses, victims and/or suspects as well as other persons that may have knowledge of or had acted in the robbery. The information may also answer questions as to the suspect(s) and witnesses whereabouts prior to this robbery as well as other investigative inquires.

Telephone Records-Affidavit
(Narcotics/Gangs/Weapons/Trafficking)

Based on my training and experience I know that narcotics/gangs/weapons trafficking is a conspiratorial scheme involving many persons. Communications between co-conspirators is most frequently accomplished by use of telecommunications devices, including pagers, traditional landline telephones and cellular telephones.

Based on my training and experience, which includes not only my own participation in narcotics/gangs/weapons trafficking investigations, but also the information I have learned from other experienced investigators in this field, I know that a review of the telephone business records maintained by the cellular telephone service provider for telecommunications devices used by narcotics/gangs/weapons traffickers has resulted in the identification of dealers, distributors, smugglers, purchasers, and money launderers using the telephone, of previously unidentified co-conspirators, locations utilized by co-conspirators in the furtherance of illegal activities and other evidence of the crimes being investigated.

Voicemail Records/Password Reset-Search Warrant

IT IS HEREBY ORDERED Metro PCS shall change the voice mail password for ###-###-#### and to further provide law enforcement officers with digital copies of all messages stored in this account at the time of execution of the warrant.

Voicemail Records/Password Reset-Affidavit

Based on my training and experience, I know that voice mail messages for a cellular telephone are maintained on the service provider's computer server and are retrievable via the suspect's cellular telephone handset. I know that co-conspirators using cellular telephones commonly receive and/or store incoming voice mail messages, including messages from other gang members and gang leaders. I believe a review of the content of conversations stored in the voice mail messages stored via the suspect's cellular telephone in this investigation will provide investigative leads and evidence relevant to this ongoing criminal investigation.

Based on my training and experience, I know that a cellular telephone subscriber/user can access his/her voice mail messages from this server by prompting a previously established password on the keypad of the cellular telephone. Based on my training and experience, I know that upon receipt of a court order commanding such action, the service provider can change the existing password (usually created by the subscriber to maintain security and protection of his voice mail messages) to a new password that, when provided to law enforcement, will allow law enforcement to access the target cellular telephone's voice mail messages. I believe a review of the content of conversations stored in the voice mails for __________ will provide investigative leads and evidence relevant to this ongoing criminal investigation.

Telephone Records-Calls to Destination-Search Warrant

A 'calls to destination' search requires all cellular telephone service providers who have been served with the search warrant to check their records for any phone calls made to a particular phone number at a certain time. For example, a school receives a bomb threat from a caller ID blocked phone number. The investigators would a search warrant to <u>every</u> communications provider in the area, cellular and landline, asking them to check if any of their customers called the school at the time the call was received. Having a narrow time frame is extremely important as a location, such as a school, may receive multiple phone calls in a very short time frame.

Another scenario where this type of search may be useful is during narcotics investigations. If an informant receives a phone call from an upper level dealer, but the caller ID is blocked, a calls to destination search will reveal the phone number that called. The suggested search warrant language is:

IT IS HEREBY ORDERED, _________ (insert name of company) conduct a calls-to-destination search of their call detail records for the period _______ to _________ (limited time frame) on _______ (date) and identify any and all _______(insert name of company) telephone numbers used to place calls to the following telephone number ________ (insert phone number that received the call).

IT IS HEREBY ORDERED, upon locating a corresponding record _______ (insert name of company) shall provide the then current subscriber information and their corresponding call detail records for incoming and outgoing calls for 30 days. _______ (insert name of company) shall also provide any other phone numbers on the same account and any other accounts billed to any subscriber at the same address as for any of the numbers located during the above search.

Calling Card-Search Warrant

For calling cards where you have the actual card:

IT IS HEREBY ORDERED __________ (insert name of calling card company) shall provide telephone call detail records (date, time, duration, originating number, and destination number,) for all calls placed using the prepaid calling card _______ (describe card) administered by __________ (insert name of calling card company) associated with the "scratch off" personal identification number ___________ (insert PIN).

If you know the suspect called an access number for a particular calling card company but don't know the PIN or the destination number:

IT IS HEREBY ORDERED_________ (insert name of Calling Card Company) shall provide telephone call detail records (date, time, duration, originating number, and destination number,) for all calls placed using their administered prepaid calling cards based on the following criteria:

All calls placed via any of the ________ (insert name of calling card company) prepaid access phone numbers: 800-555-1234 from the following origination numbers _________ (insert target phone number).

If any of the prepaid access numbers listed as being _________ (insert name of Calling Card Company) have in fact been resold to other, the company shall provide the name, address, and telephone contact information for the company they were sold to.

Unlocking an iPhone: Apple's iPhone/iPad/iPod Passcode Bypass Procedure

Apple has a number of challenges that you should be aware of and must be addressed prior to enlisting them for assistance. Foremost, Apple says it is technologically impossible for them to reset the handset security code on any device using iOS version 4.0 or later. However, they can read the raw data around the handset security code and provide investigators with the data contained on the device. Apple has a lot of requirements to send them a device and this is where the fun begins. For reasons that will become clear later, I would strongly suggest reading this entire section before embarking on the path of having Apple assist you.

Properly Identifying the Device

First, you are going to need to properly identify the device by model number, network (the cellular service provider), phone number or International Mobile Equipment Identified (IMEI) and Federal Communications Commission (FCC) ID number. To get the information from most phones you would access the settings menu on the phone. This is a bit of a problem if the handset is locked, which is probably the reason you're asking Apple for their assistance in the first place. You could always remove the battery cover but you might have noticed removing the battery cover on an Apple is not something they want you to do. Apple does not want consumers tinkering with their devices and replacing their own batteries—they want the phone sent to an Apple repair facility. Many law enforcement investigators think the numbers located on the bottom of the back cover of an Apple device are the serial numbers and/or the international mobile equipment identifier (IMEI). They are not, unless it is an iPhone 5 or greater. iPhone models 5 or greater have the IMEI inscribed on the lower part of the back cover. For all other models the numbers located at the bottom are the FCC identifiers for the model of phone and every iPhone model has the same numbers. This is one of the pieces of information you need but not the most critical.

Determine the IMEI

So if the number on the bottom back of the phone is not the IMEI, where is it? Apple came up with an ingenious method for placing the IMEI and the serial number by placing them on the bottom of the SIM card holder for the device. If you examine the top or side of an Apple device, equipped with a SIM card, you will see a small hole. This hole is used to remove the SIM card and the SIM card holder. You could use a specially designed tool for this which is available on the Internet or you could simply insert a small paper clip. Use caution because the SIM card holder can sometimes eject with surprising velocity. Once you have removed the SIM card holder you will see the SIM card held within. If you turn the holder over you will find the IMEI and the serial number imprinted in very tiny print. These are the numbers Apple needs to assist you.

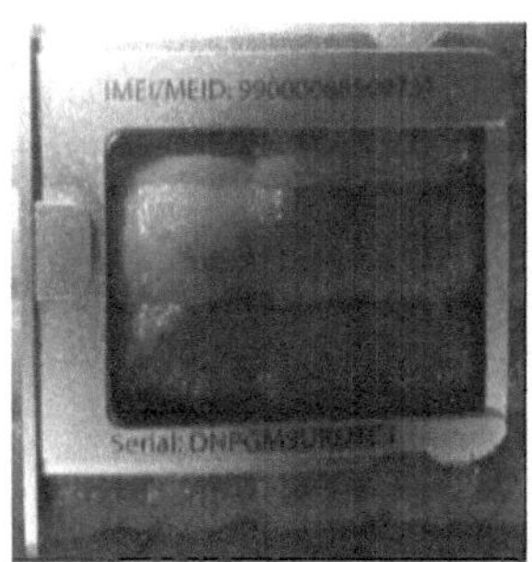

There's one small catch with this method. If the cellular service provider is Verizon you have a problem. Verizon is a CDMA network and as such many of their devices do not use SIM cards. Verizon is transitioning to GSM so some of their newer phones may have SIM card slots and SIM cards but most models do not. If there is no SIM card slot you are going to have to use some alternative methods. One method is to plug the iPhone into a computer that does NOT have iTunes installed. Once the phone is connected, Windows will detect it as a camera and the phone will show up as a connected device. **Right click** on the icon for the device and select **Properties**.

The serial number and the IMEI may be found on any packaging material and sales documents which accompanied the device when it was purchased. If all else fails you may be forced to provide Apple with the device's phone number and ask them to locate the information in their records.

Determine the Model

There are a number of variations out there. The iPhone 5 is pretty easy to identify but it can get confusing with the various models of the iPhone 3G, 3GS, 4, and 4S. An Internet search will help you confirm the physical characteristics of the phone but as a general rule these are some of the major differences between the models:

iPhone 4S:

Square in shape. Glass back. Front & back camera. Model number on back cover is A1387.

iPhone 4:

AT&T: Looks just like the iPhone 4S except the serial number on the back is A1332. It also has a SIM tray on the right side.

iPhone 4:

Verizon/Sprint: Looks just like the iPhone 4S except the serial number on the back is A1349 and it does not have a SIM card tray on the right side.

iPhone 3GS:

Plastic back. No front camera. Back text is the same shiny silver as the Apple logo.

iPhone 3G:

Looks just like the 3GS except the back text is a dull silver instead of shiny

Determine the Phone Number

First ask the suspect what the phone number is. If they won't tell you or if you are worried law enforcement interest in the device might cause them to remotely delete the contents, try calling 911 using the emergency calling feature from the lock screen. The call taker at the receiving public safety answering point should be able to tell you the number displayed on their system after you identify yourself.

The Search Warrant

Now that you have properly identified the device you can get your search warrant drafted and signed. But make no mistake about it—you do need a search warrant. Apple does not care if your suspect has a Fourth Amendment waiver permitting a warrantless search of the suspect's possessions as a condition of supervised probation or parole. You need a warrant. Not only do you need a warrant but you need to include some specialized language in the warrant in order to get Apple to cooperate. Also, Apple would like to review the warrant before it gets signed by a magistrate. This does not mean you need to send them the affidavit of probable cause supporting the warrant. They do not need to see that nor do they have the right to. What they would like to review is the section regarding the places to be searched, items to be seized, and additional instructions. As of the time of publication this is the most current language straight from Apple's legal department:

> *"It is hereby ordered that Apple Inc. assist law enforcement agents conduct the search of one Apple iOS device, Model #______________, on the ________ network with access number (phone number) __________, serial number ___________, and FCC ID#_____________; It is hereby further ordered that Apple shall provide reasonable technical assistance to enable law enforcement agents to obtain access to unencrypted data ("Data") on the Device.*

It is further ordered that, to the extent that data on the iOS device is encrypted, Apple may provide a copy of the encrypted data to law enforcement but Apple is not required to attempt to decrypt, or otherwise enable law enforcement's attempts to access any encrypted data.

Apple's reasonable technical assistance may include, but is not limited to, bypassing the iOS Device's user's passcode so that the agents may search the device, extracting data from the Device and copying the data onto an external hard drive or other storage medium that law enforcement agents may search, or otherwise circumventing the Device's security systems to allow law enforcement access to Data and to provide law enforcement with a copy of encrypted data stored on the iOS Device.

Although Apple shall make reasonable efforts to maintain the integrity of data on the Device, Apple shall not be required to maintain copies of any user data as a result of the assistance ordered herein; all evidence preservation shall remain the responsibility of law enforcement agents."

As long as you are writing all of this additional language in the search warrant you might want to consider adding not only the cellular service provider for their subscriber, call detail, and financial information, but also Apple themselves for any associated iTunes subscriber information. And as long as you are adding that you should probably also demand the contents of any iCloud backup accounts associated with the device and the subscriber.

Contact Information

The point of contact at Apple is:

Joann Chang
Apple Litigation Group
1 Infinite Loop, MS 169-2NYJ
Cupertino, CA 95014
(Phone): 408-783-0933
(Fax): 408-974-9316
joann_chang@apple.com

Waiting for Apple

Once the search warrant is signed you can fax or e-mail it to the Apple legal department. Make sure the name of the magistrate on the search warrant is legible. Do not send the device to Apple until they advise you to do so. After an internal approval process, they will contact you to schedule an appointment for the passcode bypass. They recommend that the device be delivered in person, because of a potential loss through shipping. This creates an obvious problem for investigators who work for law enforcement agencies outside of Northern California. Check with your command structure and your prosecutor's office to determine the proper steps to establish the appropriate chain of custody.

You should also be aware that, as of the time of publication, Apple's backlog was reportedly 60 days. Apparently, there is exactly one technician at Apple who performs this procedure and this is the estimated time before any newly submitted device will be examined.

Storage Media

Provided the device is running iOS4 or later, Apple requires you provide adequate storage media to enable them to provide you with a copy of the data. The storage media should be large enough to store twice the rated capacity of the device you are submitting. Considering the iPhone 5 can have up to 64 gigabytes of storage, you will need to provide them with a storage media of up to 128 gigabytes. A couple of DVDs are not going to suffice so you will likely be looking at an external hard drive to store that amount of information. Once you do obtain the evidence copy of the device's files, I would strongly recommend making a forensic copy of the file for the working version. It would be an epic mistake to start browsing through the files on the storage media returned by Apple without first making a duplicate and booking the original into evidence.

The Aftermath

After jumping through all of the hoops to properly identify the device, get the warrant drafted, reviewed, and signed, obtaining the requisite storage media, waiting two months or more for your appointment to send the evidence device in (hoping and praying it doesn't get lost), you will receive the results of the examination back from Apple. Hopefully, you take my advice and make a working copy of the files and book the original storage media into evidence.

Now that you have a working copy you open it up like a kid on Christmas morning and find...another problem. You see, when Apple reads around the handset security lock and copies the file system the resulting data is stored in their native formats; namely file types known as plists and other database files. This data is not human readable without the use of additional software to open and read the plist and database files. Not only do these files require specialized software to read but the results can be confusing.

If you've ever owned or used an iPhone and were expecting the results from Apple to appear the same as what you are used to seeing on the screen you would be horribly mistaken. For example, most people are familiar with Apple's text message screen. What they don't know if the data they are viewing is actually stored in multiple different databases. In other words, in the results sent back from Apple you might find the text message results are actually stored in multiple databases; one for the contact number, one for the message, and one for the date/time. Each set of data may be in its own file and will need to reconcile the results from the other files in order to make one coherent text message. Not only that, you will find yourself dealing with issues surrounding the date/time stamps which are in Unix or Epoch time. While the rest of the computing world calculates Unix time as the number of second from January 1st 1970, Apple calculates their times as the number of seconds from January 1st 2001. So most Unix time calculators will not work because Apple chose a different date.

Google-Assistance Unlocking an Android Cell Phone-Search Warrant

Similar to the challenges encountered with obtaining assistance from Apple, Google has also included specific language they desire in a search warrant. The following was obtained from Google's legal department:

> *To assist a law enforcement officer or agency to unlock an Android phone, Google asks that the following language (or the equivalent) be included in the search warrant:*
>
> *(i) Identify the place to be searched as the user's account identified by the IMEI/MEID number found on the back of the phone), the cellular phone and associated Gmail account, if known.*
>
> *(ii) Command the government to:*
>
> *Search and seize all stored electronic and wire communications and information in memory within the mobile device, including email, instant messaging, or other communications, and including any content that may be synchronized to or on the device from any service or application utilized by the subject as of the date of execution of the search warrant (i.e., the date of the password reset).*
>
> *(iii) With regard to Google, include the following provision:*
>
> *If necessary, and if the device can establish a data connection to the mobile network of the underlying service provider by law enforcement, Google is ordered to reactivate the Google account associated with the mobile device for the limited purpose of complying with the search warrant. Before beginning the unlock procedure, Google shall coordinate the time of executing the unlock procedure with the law enforcement officer executing the search warrant (hereafter "the law enforcement officer") to ensure all parties are prepared to conduct the device unlock.*
>
> *Google is directed to provide a single password reset for the mobile device, to provide the new password to the law enforcement officer, and upon unlocking the target mobile device, again reset the*

> *Google account password promptly upon notice from the law enforcement officer that the unlocking of the phone is complete (but in any event no longer than 15 minutes), without providing it to the law enforcement officer or agency so as to prevent future access. The reset process need not be unobtrusive to the subject and the subject may receive notice to one or more accounts of the reset as a part of this unlock process; such notice is not a violation of any seal or nondisclosure requirement.*

[NOTE: There are a couple of things to note in the preceding paragraph. One, they are going to relock the email account after sending the unlock code to the phone. This is prevent anyone from looking at the email contents without judicial authorization. As long as you are writing the warrant to reset the password you might as well include the email content. Also note that Google is telling you upfront the subject is going to be notified of the password reset. Keep that in mind. If you did not include the email content in the search warrant you may want to submit a preservation letter pursuant to 18 USC 2703(f) to preserve the emails before they get deleted. Make sure to include the preservation of any deleted or "Trash" emails. Once a Gmail user deleted an email is goes in to the trash and stays there. Those messages can be recovered. If they deleted their trash file the messages are gone and irretrievable.

> *"The law enforcement officer is prohibited from using or attempting to use the new password to attempt to access the subject's online accounts other than as synchronized on and stored in memory within the target device at the time of execution of the warrant."*

[NOTE: This is why you want to include the email contents in your search warrant.]

> *"In addition, Google's policy is to notify the user when we receive legal process on his/her account. Google will refrain from doing so if precluded by the court or upon your certification that disclosure would impede the investigation. Please include a court issued sealing order, order under 18 U.S.C. section 2705(b) or certify that notice to the user would impede your investigation."*

[NOTE: You don't need to do this if the suspect is in custody or you don't care if they get notified. But if notifying the suspect would impede the investigation use your state sealing authority, get a non-disclosure order built in to the search warrant, or get an order under 18 USC 2705(b).

Sample Affidavit Language

Pursuant to SW # _____________, which is attached and incorporated by reference (Attachment A), your affiant has been tasked with a forensic examination of a T-Mobile HTC/G-1 Android platform cellular telephone.

The device is identified as T-Mobile HTC/G-1 Android platform cell phone, Model #______, on the _______ network with access number _________, serial number _________, and FCC ID#___________ (the "cellular device").

Upon initial examination the cellular device your affiant discovered the device is locked with a pattern protected handset security code and requires a Google/Gmail user name and password to bypass the lock. At this time you affiant does not possess the equipment or training to successfully bypass this lock. To the best of your affiant's knowledge such technology does not currently exist at the Hayward Police Department or any other surrounding law enforcement agencies in Alameda County, California. Attempts to bypass the handset security lock using the existing tools and techniques available to your affiant have thus far failed.

Your affiant has have spoken to representatives from the cellular service provider and Google. Your affiant was informed by representatives from both companies the only way to unlock the phone is to have the Gmail user name and password, which was required when the device was setup. Your affiant is aware from prior law enforcement training and experience, as well as, personal experience using a cellular device with the Android operating system, when a user purchases and activates an Android operating system phone they are prompted to create or enter a Google Gmail account. The purpose of this account is to enable Google to remotely reset the handset security lock feature in the event the user forgets their original code.

Therefore, your affiant believes Google can provide the Gmail account name associated with the device, as well as, reset the password and provide a new, temporary password to you affiant or his designee. As established previously, I believe there is probable cause to believe evidence of the crime under investigation exists in the cellular device described in Exhibit 1A. In order to recover evidence of the crime under investigation your affiant requests Google be directed to provide information and technical assistance, by way of example and not limitation, including the Gmail user name associated with the device and resetting the password to the associated account.

Sample Search Warrant Language

It is hereby ordered that Google Inc. provide the username for the cellular device identified as T-Mobile HTC/G-1 Android platform cell phone, Model #________, on the ________ network with access number _________, serial number __________, and FCC ID#_____________ (the "cellular device") by providing the associated user name and by resetting the cellular devices password.

It is hereby ordered to Search and seize all stored electronic and wire communications and information in memory within the mobile device, including email, instant messaging, or other communications, and including any content that may be synchronized to or on the device from any service or application utilized by the subject as of the date of execution of the search warrant (i.e., the date of the password reset).

It is hereby ordered, If necessary, and if the device can establish a data connection to the mobile network of the underlying service provider by law enforcement, Google is ordered to reactivate the Google account associated with the mobile device for the limited purpose of complying with the search warrant. Before beginning the unlock procedure, Google shall coordinate the time of executing the unlock procedure with the law enforcement officer executing the search warrant (hereafter "the law enforcement officer") to ensure all parties are prepared to conduct the device unlock.

It is hereby ordered Google is directed to provide a single password reset for the mobile device, to provide the new password to the law enforcement officer, and upon unlocking the target mobile device, again reset the Google account password promptly upon notice from the law enforcement officer that the unlocking of the phone is complete (but in any event no longer than 15 minutes), without providing it to the law enforcement officer or agency so as to prevent future access. The reset process need not be unobtrusive to the subject and the subject may receive notice to one or more accounts of the reset as a part of this unlock process; such notice is not a violation of any seal or nondisclosure requirement.

Pen Register-Search Warrant

As defined in Section 3127 of the Federal Electronic Communications Privacy Act, the term "pen register" means a device which records or decodes electronic or other impulses which identify the numbers dialed or transmitted on the telephone line to which such device is attached. The term "trap-and-trace device" means a device which captures the incoming electronic or

other impulses which identify the originating number of an instrument or device from which a wire or electronic communication was transmitted. Thus, the installation of both a pen register and a trap-and-trace device allows law enforcement officers to determine telephone numbers being called from and to a particular telephone number.

The Federal Electronic Communications Privacy Act regulates the use of pen registers and trap- and-trace devices (18 U.S.C. Sections 3121-3126). Section 3122 expressly authorizes a state investigative or law enforcement officer to apply for an order, or an extension of an order, authorizing the installation and use of a pen register or a trap-and-trace device, in writing under oath, to a court of competent jurisdiction of the state. Section 3123 requires the applicant to justify that the information likely to be obtained is relevant to an ongoing criminal investigation (as opposed to probable cause required for a warrant). The order shall not exceed 60 days. Extensions may be granted, but only upon application, and may not exceed 60 days. The order shall direct that the order be sealed until otherwise directed by the court, and it shall direct the person owning the line or assisting in the installation not to disclose until further order of the court. An order for a pen register or trap-and-trace device may be issued by a state court of "general criminal jurisdiction"; (Cal Const. Art. VI, Section 10), so a Superior Court judge can issue an order.

No California case has discussed the propriety of obtaining such an order. However, a California Attorney General Opinion, No. 03-406, has concluded that the federal statutes governing the installation of pen registers and trap-and-trace devices do not provide authority for issuance of a state court order permitting a state law enforcement officer to install or use pen registers or trap-and-trace devices. The rationale of the Opinion is that in

California telephone call information is protected by a right of privacy so that such records may only be obtained by a law enforcement officer upon a showing of probable cause. In view of this Opinion, California state law enforcement officers should only use the federal statute if the court order includes a provision that the affidavit establishes probable cause.

A pen register and/or a trap-and-trace device may be installed if a search warrant has been obtained. (*People v. Larkin* (1987) 194 Cal.App.3d 650, 654.) In contrast to the procedure described above, the warrant is valid for only ten days pursuant to Penal Code section 1534, and the warrant must establish probable cause.

Pursuant to 18 U.S.C. § 3123, Applicant has certified that the information likely to be obtained by such use is relevant to an ongoing criminal investigation being conducted by the River City Police Department (hereinafter the "Investigative Agency") in connection with possible violations of 11378/11379 H&S by Kathleen Lama.

Pursuant to 18 U.S.C. §§ 2703(c)(1)(B) and 2703(d), Applicant has offered specific and articulable facts showing that there are reasonable grounds to believe that records or other information identifying subscribers or customers (not including the contents of communications) for telephone numbers identified through the pen register and trap and trace devices on the Target Device, changes in service regarding the Target Device, cell site information' regarding the Target Device, and records or other information pertaining to subscriber(s) or customers) (but not including the contents of communications) for the Target Device are relevant and material to an ongoing criminal investigation of the specified offenses.

THEREFORE, IT IS HEREBY ORDERED, pursuant to 18 U.S.C. § 3123, that agents of the Investigative Agency may install, or cause to be installed, and use a pen register to record or decode dialing, routing, addressing, or signaling information transmitted' from the Target Device, to record the date and time of such dialings or transmissions, and to record the length of time the telephone receiver in question is "off the hook" or connected for incoming or outgoing calls and attempts, for a period of sixty (60) days from the date this Order is filed by the Court,' provided, however, that such information shall not include the contents of any communication;

IT IS FURTHER ORDERED, pursuant to 18 U.S.C. § 3123, that agents of the Investigative Agency may install, or cause to be installed, and use a trap and trace device on the Target Device to capture and record the incoming electronic or other impulses which identify the originating numbers or other dialing, routing, addressing, or signaling information' reasonably likely to identify the source of a wire or electronic communication, and to record the date, time, and duration of calls created by such incoming impulses, for a period of sixty (60) days from the date this Order is filed by the Court, provided, however, that such information shall not include the contents of any communication;

IT IS FURTHER ORDERED that the Investigative Agency is authorized to obtain from the telephone Service Providers: (1) any cell site information that might be available when the Target Device is turned "on" but a call is not in progress; (2) information that would allow it to triangulate' multiple antenna tower locations and thereby attempt to determine the precise location of the user of the Target Device; or (3) Global Positioning System (GPS) information regarding the location of the Target Device. Provider shall, upon direction of the investigating officer or his designee, initiate a signal to determine the location of the target telephone on the service provider's network or use other reference points which may reasonably be available to assist in the location of the target telephone. This may be performed at any time of day or night, owing to the potential need to locate the target phone outside of normal business hours.

IT IS FURTHER ORDERED pursuant to 18 U.S.C. §§ 2703(c)(1)(B), 2703(c)(2), 2703(d), 3122, and 3123 that Adelphia Communications, Adelphia Long Distance, Allegiance Telecom of California, Inc., Astound, AT&T California, AT&T Local Service, AT&T Long Distance, AT&T Midwest, AT&T Nevada, AT&T Southwest, Bell South Telecommunications, Broadwing Communications, Cellco Partnership doing business as Verizon Wireless, Cellular One, Central Wireless Partnership doing business as Sprint PCS, Cingular Wireless, Comcast, Cox Communications, Dobson Cellular, Dobson Communications, Edge Wireless LLC, Electric Lightwave Inc., Ernbarq, Ernest Communications, Evans Telephone Company, Frontier: A Citizens Communications Company, Genesis Communications International, Google, ICG Communications, ICG Telecom Group, Locus Communications, Metrocall, Metro PCS, Mpower,

Nationwide Paging, Navigator Telecommunications LLC, Network Services LLC, Nextel Communications, NIX Communications, Pac West Telecomm Incorporated, Qwest Communications, RCN Communications, Roseville Telephone Company, Slcype, Sprint-Nextel, TelePacific Communications, Teligent, Time-Warner Telecom, T-Mobile USA Inc., TracFone Wireless, USA Mobility, US Cellular, US TelePacific Corp. doing business as TelePacific Communications, Verizon California, Verizon District of Columbia, Verizon Maryland, Verizon New Jersey, Verizon New York, Verizon Northwest, Verizon Texas, Virgin Mobile, Vonage, Weblink Wireless, West Coast PCS LLC doing business as Sure West Wireless, Western Wireless Corporation, X0 Communications, and any and all other telephone service providers (including any Internet service provider or other electronic communications provider providing voice-over IP telephony [VoIP (collectively, "the Telephone Service Providers"), and any and all other persons or entities providing wire or electronic communications service in the United States whose assistance may facilitate the execution of this Order, shall disclose or provide, upon oral or written demand by agents of the Investigative Agency:

1.   For the Target Device, records or other information pertaining to subscriber(s) or customer(s), including cell site information and toll or call detail records (including in two-way radio feature mode) for the sixty (60) days prior to the date this Order is filed by the Court (but not including the contents of communications);

2.   For the Target Device, after receipt and storage, records or other information pertaining to subscriber(s) or customer(s), including (1) the means and source of payment for the service and (2) cell site information, provided to the United States for (a) the origination of a call from the Target Device or the answer of a call to the Target Device and (b) the termination of the call (but not including the contents of the communications);

3.   Pursuant to 18 U.S.C. § 2703(c), after receipt and storage, the following subscriber records and other information for all published, non-published, or unlisted dialing, routing, addressing, or signaling information captured by the pen register and trap and trace device on the Target Device:
    (i)   name;
    (ii)   address;

(iii)   local and long distance telephone connection records, or records of session times and durations with Target Device;

(iv)   length of service (including start date) and types of service utilized; and

(v)   telephone or instrument number or other subscriber number or identity, including any temporarily assigned network address; and

4.   Any and all changes (including additions, deletions, and transfers) in service regarding the Target Device, including telephone numbers; other unique identifiers such as Electronic Serial Numbers (ESNs), Subscriber Identity Modules (SIMs), International Mobile Subscriber Identifiers (IMSIs), International Mobile station Equipment Identities (IMEIs), and/or Urban Fleet Mobile Identifiers (UFMIs); and subscriber information (published, non-published, listed, or unlisted) associated with these service changes.

IT IS FURTHER ORDERED that this authorization for the installation and use of a pen register and trap and trace device applies not only to the Target Device, but also to any changed telephone numbers subsequently assigned to an instrument bearing the. same ESN, SIM, IMSI, IMEI, and/or UFMI as the Target Device, or any changed ESN, SIM, IMSI, IMEI; and/or UFMI subsequently assigned to the same telephone number as the Target Device, and any additional changed telephone number, ESN, SIM, IMSI, IMEI, and/or UFMI, whether the changes occur consecutively or simultaneously, listed to the same subscriber or account number as the Target Device within the 60-day period authorized by this Order and further, that, pursuant to 18 U.S.C. § 3123(b)(1)(C), the tracing operations authorized by this Order be without geographical limits.

IT IS FURTHER ORDERED that the Target Device's Telephone Service Providers shall furnish the results of the pen register and trap and trace devices to agents of the Investigative Agency as soon as practicable, twenty four (24) hours a day for the duration of the Order.

IT IS FURTHER ORDERED that the Target Device's Telephone Service Providers be reasonably compensated by the Investigative Agency for reasonable expenses directly incurred in providing information, facilities, and assistance.

IT IS FURTHER ORDERED, pursuant to 18 U.S.C. §§ 2705(b) and 3123(d), that this Order and the Application be SEALED until otherwise ordered by the Court, that the identity of any targets of the investigation and the possible violations thereof may be redacted from any copy of the Order served on any service provider or other person, and that the Target Device's Telephone Service Providers and any other Telephone Service Provider which provides service to a telephone number that either places telephone calls to, or receives telephone calls from, the Target Device, shall not disclose in any manner, directly or indirectly, by any action or inaction, the existence of this Order, in full or redacted form, of the pen register or trap and trace devices, or of this investigation, to the listed subscribers for the Target Device, or to any other person unless otherwise ordered by this Court.

IT IS FURTHER ORDERED that night service of this order is authorized, owing to the need to utilize one or more provisions of this Order outside of normal business hours.

IT IS FURTHER ORDERED, this Order shall remain in effect from 5/8/2013 through 7/7/2013.

Pen Register for PCTDD-Affidavit

Post cut through dialed digits (PCTDD) are any key pressed after the completion of the call. For example, a suspect who calls an 800 phone number to access their calling card will be required to enter the PIN and the phone number to be dialed. Without a pen register it is extremely difficult to obtain the PIN and dialed number. Some jurisdictions consider this content, similar to a text message, and require a Title III wiretap to obtain it; while others allow it to be obtained through the use of a pen register. Check with your legal advisor regarding the legality of collecting PCTDD

Based on my training an experience I know it is nearly impossible to obtain outgoing phone calls when the call is routed through a prepaid phone card without the use of a pen register. The only other alternative known to your affiant is to identify the personal identification number (PIN) printed on the card and seek an additional Court Order for phone records made on that particular prepaid calling card. This requires accessing the actual physical card and would be extremely difficult without alerting the suspect to law enforcement's interest.

Application for Electronic Communications Interception

UNITED STATES DISTRICT COURT

___________DISTRICT OF____________

IN THE MATTER OF THE APPLICATION)
OF THE UNITED STATES OF AMERICA FOR)
AN ORDER AUTHO~IZING THE INTERCEPTION)
OF ELECTRONIC COMMUNICATIONS)

APPLICATION FOR INTERCEPTION OF ELECTRONIC
COMMUNICATIONS

_______________, Assistant United States Attorney_____________________, District of_______________/Special Attorney, United States Department of Justice, being duly sworn, states:

1.   I am an investigative or law enforcement officer of the United States within the meaning of Section 2510(7) of Title 18, United States Code, that is, an attorney authorized by law to prosecute or participate in the prosecution of United States federal felony offenses. I am also an attorney for the Government as defined in Rule l(b) (1) of the Federal Rules of Criminal Procedure, and, therefore, pursuant to Section 2516 (3)of Title 18, United States Code, I am authorized to make an application to a Federal judge of competent jurisdiction for an order authorizing the interception of electronic communications.

2.   This application is for an order pursuant to Section 2518 of Title 18, United States Code, authorizing the interception of electronic communications for a thirty (30) day period of (name the interceptees) and others as yet unknown to (and from) the (telephone/digital-display paging device (s)/facsimile machine/computer/internet account number_____________) (bearing or using the telephone number(s)___________ ,subscribed to by__________) concerning federal felony offenses, that is, offenses involving violations of (list the section(s) of the United States Code and briefly describe the applicable offense(s)) .

3.	I have discussed all of the circumstances of the above offenses with Special Agent___________ of the______________, who has directed and conducted this investigation, and have examined the Affidavit of Special Agent______________ of this date (attached to this application as Exhibit__, and which is incorporated by reference). Whereof your applicant states upon information and belief that:

    a.	there is probable cause to believe that (name the violators) have committed, are committing and will continue to commit violations of (list the offenses);

    b.	there is probable cause to believe that particular electronic communications of (name the interceptee/s) concerning the above-described offenses will be obtained through the interception for which authorization is here in applied. In particular, there is probable cause to believe that the communications to be intercepted will concern the telephone numbers of associates of (name the violators) and the dates, times and places for commission of the aforementioned federal felony offenses when (name the interceptee/s) communicate with their co-conspirators, aiders and abettors, and other participants in the conspiracy, thereby identifying the co-conspirators and aiders and abettors of (name the violators) and others as yet unknown, their places of operation. In addition, these communications are expected to constitute admissible evidence of the above-described offenses;

    c.	normal investigative procedures have been tried and have failed, reasonably appear to be unlikely to succeed if tried, or are too dangerous to employ, as are described in further detail in the attached affidavit of Special Agent and

    d.	there is probable cause to believe that (list the facilities from which, or the place where, the electronic communications are to be intercepted) are being, and will continue to be used in connection with the commission of the above-described offenses.

The attached affidavit contains a full and complete statement of facts concerning all previous applications that have been made to any judge of competent jurisdiction for authorization to intercept, or for approval of interception of wire, oral or electronic communications involving any of the same individuals, facilities, or places specified in this application.

On the basis of the allegations contained in this application and on the basis of the attached affidavit of Special Agent_____________________.

IT IS HEREBY REQUESTED that this Court issue an order, pursuant to the power conferred on it by Section 2518 of Title 18, United States Code, authorizing the (name the investigative agency/agencies) to intercept electronic communications to (and from) the above-described (telephone/digital display paging device, facsimile machine, computer, internet account), and providing that such interceptions not terminate automatically after the first interception that reveals the manner in which the alleged co-conspirators and others as yet unknown conduct their illegal activities, but continue until all communications are intercepted which reveal fully the manner in which the above-named persons and others as yet unknown are committing the offenses described herein, and which reveal fully the identities of their confederates, their places of operation, and the nature of the conspiracy involved therein, or for a period of thirty(30) days measured from the day on which investigative or law enforcement officers first begin to conduct an interception under this Court's order or ten (10) days after this order is entered, whichever is earlier.

IT IS REQUESTED FURTHER that in the event that the target facility is transferred outside the territorial jurisdiction of this Court, interceptions may take place in any other jurisdiction within the United States.

IT IS REQUESTED FURTHER that this Court issue an order pursuant to Section 2518(4) of Title 18, United States Code, directing that (list the communications service provider(s)), a communication service provider as defined in Section 2510(15) of Title 18, United States Code, shall furnish, and continue to furnish, the applicant and investigative agency with all information, facilities and technical assistance necessary to accomplish the interceptions unobtrusively and with a minimum of interference with the services that such providers are according the persons whose communications are to be intercepted, and to ensure an effective and secure installation of electronic devices capable of interception of electronic communications to (and from) the above-described (telephone/digital display paging device/facsimile machine/computer/internet account), with the service provider to be compensated by the applicant for reasonable expenses incurred in providing such facilities or assistance.

IT IS REQUESTED FURTHER that, to avoid prejudice to this criminal investigation, the Court order the said providers of electronic communication service and their agents and employees not to disclose or cause a disclosure of this Court's order or the request for information, facilities and assistance by the(identify the investigative agency/agencies) or the existence of the investigation to any person other than those of their agents and employees who require said information to accomplish the services hereby requested. In particular, said providers and87their agents and employees should be ordered not to make such disclosure to a lessee, telephone subscriber, or any interceptee or participant in the intercepted communications.

IT IS REQUESTED FURTHER that this Court direct that this order be executed as soon as practicable after it is signed and that all monitoring of communications shall be recorded and examined by monitoring agents or attorneys to determine the relevance of the intercepted electronic communications to the pending investigation and that the disclosure of the contents or nature of the electronic communications intercepted be limited to those communications relevant to the pending investigation, in accordance with the minimization requirements of Chapter 119 of Title 18, United States Code. The interception of communications authorized by this Court's order must terminate upon attainment of the authorized objectives or, in any event, at the end of thirty (30) days measured from the earlier of the day on which investigative or law enforcement officers first begin to conduct an interception under this Court's order or ten (10) days after the order is entered, whichever is earlier.

IT IS REQUESTED FURTHER that the Court order that either Assistant United States Attorney/Special Attorney_______________, or any other Assistant United States Attorney/Special Attorney familiar with the facts of this case, provide to the Court a report on or about the (tenth), (twentieth) and (thirtieth) days following the date of this order showing what progress has been made toward achievement of the authorized objectives and the need for continued interception. If any of the aforementioned reports should become due on a weekend or holiday,

IT IS REQUESTED FURTHER that such report become due on the next business day thereafter.

IT IS REQUESTED FURTHER that the Court order that its orders, this application and the accompanying affidavit and proposed order(s), and all interim reports filed with the Court with regard to this matter be sealed until further order of this Court, except that copies of the order(s), in full or redacted form, may be served on the (identify the investigative agency/agencies) and the service provider(s) as necessary to effectuate the Court's order as set forth in the proposed order(s) accompanying this application.

Affidavit for Electronic Communications Interception

UNITED STATES DISTRICT COURT
____________DISTRICT OF_____________

IN THE MATTER OF THE APPLICATION)
OF THE UNITED STATES OF AMERICA)
FOR AN ORDER AUTHORIZING THE) MISC. NO.
INTERCEPTION OF ELECTRONIC)
COMMUNICATIONS)

AFFIDAVIT IN SUPPORT OF APPLICATION

___________________, being duly sworn, deposes and states as follows:

1. I am a Special Agent with the United States Department of Justice. I have been so employed by the___________ for the past ( ) years. I have participated in investigations involving (organized crime/drug trafficking, etc.) activities for the past( ) years. (Describe present assignment)

2. I am an investigative or law enforcement officer of the United States within the meaning of Section 2510(7) of Title 18, United States Code, in that I am empowered by law to conduct investigations and to make arrests for federal felony offenses.

3. This affidavit is submitted in support of an application for an order authorizing the interception of electronic communications occurring (specify the facility or facilities to which the application and affidavit are directed).

4. I have participated in the investigation of the above offenses. As a result of my personal participation in this investigation, through interviews with and analysis of reports submitted by other (Special Agents of the ___________and/or other state/local law enforcement personnel), and by the analysis of

(surveillance logs/pen register information, etc.), I am familiar with all aspects of this investigation. On the basis of this familiarity, and on the basis of other information which I have reviewed and determined to be reliable, I allege that:

a. There is probable cause to believe that (list the violators) have committed, are committing, and will continue to commit (list the offense(s) - can be any federal felony offense).

b. There is probable cause to believe that particular electronic communications of (list the interceptees) concerning the above offenses will be obtained through the interception of such communications to (and from) the (telephone/digital pager/facsimile machine/computer/internet account) (assigned/using/bearing account/telephone number/s________________), subscribed to by____________(and if applicable, the facility's physical location)). In particular, there is probable cause to believe that the communications to be intercepted will concern the (telephone numbers of associates of (list the violator(s)) and the dates, times, places, and plans for commission of the aforementioned federal felony offenses when (list the interceptees) communicate with their co-conspirators, aiders and abettors, and other participants in the conspiracy, thereby identifying the co-conspirators and aiders and abettors of(the violators), and others as yet unknown, their places of operation, (etc.). In addition, these communications are expected to constitute admissible evidence of the above-described offenses.

c. Normal investigative procedures have been tried and have failed, reasonably appear to be unlikely to succeed if tried, or are too dangerous to employ, as is described herein in further detail.

d. There is probable cause to believe that (list the facilities over which the electronic communications are to be intercepted) are being, and will continue to be, used in connection with the commission of the above offenses.

PERSONS EXPECTED TO BE INTERCEPTED

Include a short description of each expected interceptee; if appropriate, explain why certain participants in the offenses are not expected to be interceptees.

FACTS AND CIRCUMSTANCES

Provide an in-depth discussion of the facts in support of the probable cause statements above. If informant information provides a basis for any of the probable cause for any of the required information, provide adequate qualifying language for each informant.

(In drug cases, if appropriate, include a "facts and circumstances" paragraph regarding use of pagers, e.g., "I know from my training, experience, and discussions with other experienced agents that narcotics traffickers frequently use paging devices to further their illicit business. Pagers permit co-conspirators to contact each other with virtually no possibility that their communications will be intercepted. For example, the type of paging device used in this matter allows a conspirator to signal a confederate, identify himself through a numerical code, and convey the number of a secure or non-suspect telephone, usually a pay telephone, at which he can be contacted. The conspirator receiving this information can then go to a secure or non-suspect telephone, return the call, and engage in a criminal discussion with his confederate which, under normal circumstances, will be incapable of interception by law enforcement authorities.")

NORMAL INVESTIGATIVE PROCEDURES

Need for Electronic Interception

Based upon your affiant's training and experience, as well as the experience of other (list the Special Agents of the and/or state/local officers of), and based upon all of the facts set forth herein, it is your affiant's belief that the interception of electronic communications is the only available technique with a reasonable likelihood of securing the evidence necessary to prove beyond a reasonable doubt that (list the violator/s), and others as yet unknown are engaged in the above-described offenses.

Numerous investigative procedures that are usually employed in the investigation of this type of criminal case have been tried and have failed, reasonably appear to be unlikely to succeed if they are tried, or are too dangerous to employ.(Include a discussion of the details of specific problems regarding the use of alternative investigative techniques in this investigation. Then discuss the standard problem areas, as synopsized below, modifying the statements to comport with the actual circumstances of your case.)

<u>Physical Surveillance</u>

Physical surveillance has been attempted on many occasions in this investigation. Although it has proven valuable in identifying some of the targets' activities and associates, physical surveillance, if not used in conjunction with other techniques, including electronic surveillance is of limited value. Even if highly successful, physical surveillance does not always succeed in gathering evidence of the criminal activity under investigation. It is an investigative technique used to confirm meetings between alleged conspirators, and usually only leads investigators to speculate as to the purpose of the meeting(s). It is also a technique used to corroborate information obtained from confidential informants. Further, physical surveillance of the alleged conspirators will not establish conclusively the elements of the subjects' violations and has not and most likely will not establish conclusively the identities of various conspirators. Prolonged or regular physical surveillance of the targets would most likely be noticed, causing them to become more cautious in their illegal activities, to flee to avoid further investigation and prosecution, to cause a threat to the safety of the informant(s) and undercover agent(s), or otherwise to compromise the investigation.

With regard to this investigation, physical surveillance is unlikely to establish conclusively the roles of the named conspirators, to identify additional conspirators, to identify the conspirators' sources of supply, or otherwise to provide admissible evidence in regard to this investigation because (provide details of any of the following, as applicable) :

- Conspirators are using counter-surveillance, such as erratic driving behavior in order to detect surveillance; or have evinced that they suspect law enforcement surveillance of their activities;

- The nature of the neighborhood forecloses physical surveillance (e.g., a close-knit community; cul-de-sac, dead end, or large apartment building; and/or the neighbors all know each other and call the police when surveillance is spotted) ;

- Further surveillance would only serve to alert the conspirators of the law enforcement interest in their activities and compromise the investigation.

<u>Use of Grand Jury Subpoenas</u>

Based upon your affiant's experience and conversations with Assistant United States Attorneys for the_______________ District of_____________ who have experience prosecuting violations of criminal law, your affiant believes that subpoenaing persons who are believed to be involved in this conspiracy, or their associates before a Federal Grand Jury would most likely not be completely successful in achieving the stated goals of this investigation. The targets of this investigation, and their co-conspirators and other participants, should they be called to testify before the Grand Jury, would most likely be uncooperative and invoke their Fifth Amendment privilege not to testify. It93would then be unwise to seek any kind of immunity for any of these persons because the granting of such immunity might foreclose prosecution of the most culpable members of this conspiracy, and could not ensure that such immunized witnesses would provide truthful testimony before the Grand Jury. Additionally, the service of Grand Jury subpoenas upon the targets or their co-conspirators would only alert the targets to the existence of this investigation, thereby causing them to become more cautious in their activities, to flee to avoid further investigation or prosecution, to threaten the lives of the informant(s) and the undercover agent(s), or otherwise to compromise this investigation.

(Add specific information about any persons who have been subpoenaed before the Grand Jury, especially when the Fifth Amendment was invoked or when the witness later advised the targets.)

<u>Confidential Informants and Cooperating Sources</u>

Reliable confidential informants/cooperating sources have been developed and used, and will continue to be developed and used, in regard to this investigation, but these sources (discuss those that are applicable) :

-	exist on the fringe of this organization and, therefore, have no direct contact with mid- or high-level members of the organization, or such contact is virtually impossible because the sources have no need to communicate with such individuals,

-	refuse to testify before the Grand Jury or at trial because of a fear for personal or family safety; or their testimony would be uncorroborated or otherwise subject to impeachment (due to prior record, criminal involvement, etc.);

-	are no longer associated with the targets of this investigation and their information is included for historical purposes only.

None of the confidential informants described in this affidavit are able to furnish information that would identify fully all members of this ongoing criminal conspiracy or define the roles of those conspirators sufficiently for prosecution or that would identify sufficiently (the source(s) of supply or all details of delivery, quantities, financial arrangements, and the like), etc.

Your affiant believes that information provided by the confidential sources, even if all sources agreed to testify, would not, without the evidence available through the requested electronic surveillance, result in a successful prosecution of all of the participants.

Undercover Police Officers and Agents

Undercover police officers and/or agents have been unable to infiltrate the inner workings of this conspiracy due to the close and secretive nature of this organization. Your affiant believes that there are no undercover officers/agents who can infiltrate the conspiracy at a level high enough to identify all members of the conspiracy or otherwise satisfy all the goals of this investigation. (Indicate if infiltration is not feasible because the confidential informant(s) is not in a position to make introductions of undercover officers to mid- or high-level members of the organization.)

(Details of the use of undercover officers should have been provided in the body of this affidavit, with this section indicating the limitations of such usage.)

Interviews of Subjects or Associates

Based upon your affiant's experience, your affiant believes that interviews of subjects or their known associates would produce insufficient information concerning the identities of all of the persons involved in the conspiracy, the source of the drugs, financing, etc., the location of records, drugs, etc., or other pertinent information regarding the subject crimes. Your affiant also believes that any responses to the interviews would contain a significant number of half-truths and untruths, diverting the investigation with false leads or otherwise frustrating the investigation. Additionally, such interviews would likely result in non-targeted interviewees alerting the members of the conspiracy, thereby compromising the investigation and resulting in the possible destruction or concealment of (documents) (other evidence) and the possibility of harm to cooperating source(s), the identity of whom may become known or whose existence may otherwise be compromised.

(This portion of the affidavit is sometimes merged with the discussion regarding the use of the Federal Grand Jury. Any actual interviews conducted, and any resulting problems should also be discussed here.)

Search Warrants

The execution of search warrants in this matter has been considered. However, use of such warrants would, in all likelihood, not yield a considerable quantity of narcotics or relevant documents, nor would the searches conducted pursuant to such warrants be likely to reveal the total scope of the criminal operation and the identities of the co-conspirators. (It is unlikely that all, or even many, of the principals of this organization would be at anyone location when a search warrant was executed.) Your affiant believes that search warrants executed at this time would be more likely to compromise the investigation by alerting the principals of the investigation, thereby, allowing unidentified co-conspirators to insulate themselves further from successful detection, as well as to otherwise frustrate the purposes of this investigation. (If search warrants were executed, then discuss the results and why this information is not enough to satisfy the goals of the investigation.)

<u>Pen Registers/Telephone Tolls/Trap and Trace</u>

Telephone toll/pen register/trap and trace information has been used in this investigation, as described above. (Provide a synopsis of the results obtained from a review of these phone records; describe why this information is insufficient to identify fully other coconspirators or fulfill the needs of the investigation.)

<u>Other Limitations</u>

(Provide details as to violence (murdered or hurt witnesses, threats, etc.) and other situations present in this investigation that limit the effectiveness of normal investigative techniques.) Based upon the foregoing, it is your affiant's belief that the interception of electronic communications is an essential investigative means in obtaining evidence of the totality of the offenses in which the subject(s) and others as yet unknown are involved.

PRIOR APPLICATIONS

Based upon a check of the records of the Federal Bureau of Investigation, (and any other pertinent agency) no prior applications for an order authorizing the interception of wire, oral or electronic communications have been made involving the persons, premises or facilities named herein. If the facts warrant, include additional information concerning prior or ongoing electronic surveillance, (person named, court that issued the order, date and relevance, if any, to the current investigation.)

CONCLUSION

Your affiant believes that the facts alleged herein establish that the targets of this investigation are engaged in an ongoing criminal enterprise and that the evidence sought will be intercepted on a continuing basis following the first receipt of the particular communications that are the object of this request. Therefore, it is requested that the interception not be required to terminate when the communications described herein are first intercepted, but be allowed to continue until communications are intercepted which fully reveal the scope of the enterprise, including the identities of all participants, their places and methods of operation, and the various criminal activities in which they are engaged which are in furtherance of the enterprise, not to exceed thirty (30) days measured from the earlier of the day on which investigative or law enforcement officers first begin to conduct an interception under this Court's Order or ten (10) days after the Order is entered.

____

(NAME)
Special Agent
(Agency)

Order for Interception of Electronic Communications

UNITED STATES DISTRICT COURT

___________DISTRICT OF___________

IN THE MATTER OF THE APPLICATION   )

OF THE UNITED STATES OF AMERICA FOR   )

AN ORDER AUTHORIZING THE INTERCEPTION   )

OF ELECTRONIC COMMUNICATIONS   )

ORDER AUTHORIZING THE INTERCEPTION

OF ELECTRONIC COMMUNICATIONS

Application under oath having been made before me by_______________, Assistant United States Attorney _______________,District of_______________, /Special Attorney, United States Department of Justice, an "investigative or law enforcement officer" of the United States within the meaning of Section 2510(7) of Title 18, United States Code, and an attorney for the Government as defined in Rule l(b) (1) of the Federal Rules of Criminal Procedure, for an Order authorizing the interception of electronic communications pursuant to Section 2518 of Title 18,United States Code, and full consideration having been given to the matter set forth therein, the Court finds:

      a.   There is probable cause to believe that (list the violators) have committed, are committing, and will continue to commit violations of (list the offenses - can be any federal felony offense) ;

      b.   There is probable cause to believe that particular electronic communications of (list the interceptees) concerning the above-described offenses will be obtained through the interception for which authorization is herein applied. In particular, there is probable cause to believe that the communications to be intercepted will concern the telephone numbers of associates of (the violator/s) and the dates, times, places and plans for commission of the aforementioned federal felony offenses when (list the interceptee/s) communicate with their co-conspirators, aiders and abettors and other participants in the conspiracy, thereby identifying the co-conspirators and others as yet unknown, their places of operation, (etc.). In addition, these communications are expected to constitute admissible evidence of the above-described offenses;

c.				It has been established adequately that normal investigative procedures have been tried and have failed, reasonably appear to be unlikely to succeed if tried, or are too dangerous to employ;

d.			There is probable cause to believe that (list the facilities over which the electronic communications are to be intercepted) have been, are being and will continue to be used in connection with the commission of the above-described offenses.

WHEREFORE, IT IS HEREBY ORDERED that Special Agents of the (name the investigative agency/agencies) are authorized to intercept electronic communications over the above-described facilities.

PROVIDED that such interception(s) shall not terminate automatically after the first interception that reveals the manner in which the alleged co-conspirators and others as yet unknown conduct their illegal activities, but may continue until all communications are intercepted which fully reveal the manner in which the above-named persons and others as yet unknown are committing the offenses described herein, and which reveal fully the identities of their confederates, their places of operation, and the nature of the conspiracy involved therein, or for a period of thirty (30) days measured from the day on which investigative or law enforcement officers first begin to conduct an interception under this Order or ten (10) days after this Order is entered, whichever is earlier.

IT IS ORDERED FURTHER that, pursuant to 18 U.S.C. § 2518(3), in the event that the target facility is transferred outside the territorial jurisdiction of this court, interceptions may take place in any other jurisdiction within the United States.

IT IS ORDERED FURTHER that, based upon the request of the Applicant pursuant to Section 2518(4) of Title 18, United States Code, (name the communication service provider/s), communication service provider(s) as defined in Section 2510(15) of Title 18,United States Code, shall furnish, and continue to furnish, the Applicant and the investigative agency/agencies with all information, facilities, and technical assistance necessary to accomplish the interceptions unobtrusively and with a minimum of interference with the services that such provider(s) is according the persons whose communications are to be intercepted, with the service provider(s) to be compensated by the Applicant for reasonable expenses incurred in providing such facilities or assistance.

IT IS ORDERED FURTHER that, to avoid prejudice to the Government's criminal investigation, the above provider(s) of electronic communication service and its agents and employees are ordered not to disclose or cause a disclosure of this Order or the request for information, facilities, and assistance by the (name the investigative agency/agencies) or the existence of the investigation to any person other than those of its agents and employees who require said information to accomplish the services hereby ordered. In particular, said provider(s) and its agents and employees shall not make such disclosure to a lessee, telephone or paging device subscriber or any interceptee or participant in the intercepted communications.

IT IS ORDERED FURTHER that this Order shall be executed as soon as practicable and that all monitoring of the electronic communications shall be recorded and examined by the monitoring agents or attorneys to determine the relevance of the intercepted electronic communications to the pending investigation and that the disclosure of the contents or nature of the electronic communications intercepted be limited to those communications relevant to the pending investigation, in accordance with the minimization requirements of Chapter 119 of Title 18, United States Code. The interception of communications must terminate upon the attainment of the authorized objectives, not to exceed thirty (30) days measured from the earlier of the day on which investigative or law enforcement officers first begin to conduct an interception under this Order or ten (10) days after the Order is entered.

IT IS ORDERED FURTHER that Assistant United States Attorney/Special Attorney____________ or any other Assistant United States Attorney/Special Attorney familiar with the facts of this case shall provide this Court with a report on or about the (tenth), (twentieth) and (thirtieth) days following the date of this Order showing what progress has been made toward achievement of the authorized objectives and the need for continued interception. If any of the above-ordered reports should become due on a weekend or holiday, IT IS ORDERED FURTHER that such report shall become due on the next business day thereafter.

IT IS ORDERED FURTHER that this Order, the application, affidavit, and proposed Order(s), and all interim reports filed with this Court with regard to this matter shall be sealed until further order of this Court, except that copies of the Order(s), in full or redacted form, may be served on the (investigative agency/agencies) and the service provider(s) as necessary to effectuate this Order.101

UNITED STATES DISTRICT COURT JUDGE

(District)

The Search Warrant: Property Crimes, Fraud, and Forgery

Stolen Property-Search Warrant

The description should specify the stolen property involved with reasonable particularity. Merely stating "stolen property" is insufficient. Whenever possible, the description should include the type, make or manufacturer of the stolen item, serial number, size, color, height, weight, shape, etc. Crime victims may assist the police in the execution of a valid search warrant and point out stolen items for the officers to seize. However, only peace officers may actually seize items.

If the list of the stolen items is extensive, a copy of a police report containing an inventory of the stolen property can be attached.

. . . the items of personal property designated Item No. 1 through Item No. 30 on the three page River City Police Department Stolen Property Report bearing Report Number 2012-123456 attached hereto and incorporated as Exhibit No. 1.

If an item of stolen property cannot be adequately described, a photograph or drawing of the item can be attached.

. . . a platinum ring with a two-carat emerald in the center, surrounded by three-leaf clusters of smaller diamonds, as shown on the hand of the woman in the photograph attached hereto and incorporated as Exhibit No. 1.

Utility Theft - Electrical Meter-Search Warrant

All items used in the theft or bypass of metering equipment such as, any illegal electrical jumpers, electrical connections, electrical wiring, and electrical conduit from the residence and/or business to utility service lines or other means bypassing the electrical meter which measures and records the amount of electricity used, and any crimping tool and lead seals used in securing the electrical meter on the property, River City electrical meter(s) or any other electrical meter(s) on the property. Fingerprints from the meter and around the meter, which may show tampering of the meter. Also to be searched for and inspection conducted thereof, electrical appliances and equipment contained within the residence and/or business and exterior land of the property known as (address), (city), California (zip code) in the County of River City.

Utility Theft - Electrical Meter-Affidavit

Based upon your Affiant's training, experience and conversations that your Affiant had with other Law Enforcement Officers and/or reports that your Affiant has read, your Affiant knows that utility services can be illegally used and that it is necessary to go to the location to determine and record the illegal use of the utilities. During the service of the Search Warrant fingerprints should be taken from the meters and around the meters to determine and link the illegal service usage.

Vehicle Theft – General/Chop Shop-Search Warrant

Stolen vehicles and/or stolen vehicle component parts, vehicles and/or components from which identifying numbers have been removed, vehicle identification number (VIN) plates, vehicle license plates and/or vehicle registration documents. Any tools tending to show vehicle VIN switching; such as; rivets, rivet guns, and die stamps. Tools tending to show the dismantling and refurbishing of vehicles; such as; cutting torches, power saws, air cutting tools, paint, paint guns, masking paper and/or sand paper. Any records/documents, address books and telephone records tending to show where additional stolen vehicles have been stolen, concealed, sold to, or the identity of other involved parties. Articles of personal property tending to show the identity of persons in control of the premises, such as; bank records, utility and rent receipts.

Vehicle Theft - Chop Shop / VIN Switching Location-Search Warrant

Vehicle Code section 2805 permits peace officers whose primary responsibility is vehicle theft investigations to conduct warrantless inspections of auto repair facilities, parking lots, dismantling facilities, body shops and similar facilities for the purpose of examining the autos and registration documents in order to find stolen cars and parts. As long as the inspected premises constitute a commercial enterprise as contemplated by section 2805, the business owner and his employees are on notice that they cannot expect to be free from periodic inspection.

All records of vehicle purchases and sales, records of purchase of component parts of vehicles, all Department of Motor Vehicle records and forms, names and addresses of customers, a (Vehicle Description) bearing a California license plate number of (License Plate #) and a vehicle identification number of (VIN #); tools used in replacing ignitions; items used to steal cars such as slim jims, filed down fingernail files and modified keys; tools used to switch Vehicle Identification Numbers (VIN) including rivets, rivet guns, die stamp equipment and VIN plates; tools for vehicle dismantling including cutting torches, engine hoists, metal cutting saws and mechanical hand tools; papers, documents and effects which tend to show dominion and control over said location, including fingerprints, handwritings, documents and effects which bear a form of identification such as a person's name, photograph, social security number and/or driver's license number, and to intercept incoming phone calls during execution of this Search Warrant. Property from vehicles parked at the said location, to wit: evidence of ownership including vehicle identification numbers, license plate numbers, engine numbers and documents bearing such numbers and/or a person's name. Property from persons, to wit: evidence of identification, vehicle registration information, keys to vehicles, and documentation related to the purchase, sale or transfer of vehicles.

Vehicle Theft - Stolen Vehicle and/or Component Parts Known

The following vehicle(s) and/or its component parts: (Vehicle Description). Any records/documents such as address books and/or telephone records that tend to show where additional stolen vehicles have been stolen, concealed, sold, purchased, and/or the identity of other involved parties. Records of storage locations, vehicle purchases and sales; all Department of Motor Vehicle records, names and addresses of person(s) to whom vehicles have been sold; tools used to dismantle vehicles; VIN plates and numbers; articles of personal property documents and effects which tend to show dominion and control over said residence/business such as bank records, utility and rent receipts, fingerprints, handwritings, and other documents or effects which bear a form of identification such as a person's name, photograph, social security number or driver's license number; and to intercept incoming phone calls during execution of this Search Warrant.

Vehicle Theft - General-Affidavit

Based upon your Affiant's training, experience and conversations that your Affiant had with other Law Enforcement Officers and/or reports that your Affiant has read, your Affiant knows that stolen vehicles and stolen vehicle component are stored with numerous items are used in the stealing and alteration of stolen vehicles and equipment. Records and documents are frequently maintained in the sale and altering of stolen vehicles and equipment. These records can identify whom the vehicles had been stolen and/or concealed from, sold to, and the identity of the parties involved. At the location articles of personal property can tend to show the identity of persons in control of the location(s). The location needs to have dominion and control completed during the service of the Search Warrant to determine who has control of the location or who is working at the location. Fingerprinting should be conducted during the service of the Search Warrant in an attempt to determine the persons violating. Frequently the involved persons and/or who purchased the stolen vehicles name(s), photograph(s), Social Security card number and/or driver's license number can be located at the location. Other evidence from the stolen vehicles may be located at the site.

Identity Theft – Computers, Credit Cards, Checks, and Identification-Search Warrant

Any items commonly used to manufacture, alter, counterfeit, prepare and/or foster the forging of checks, credit cards, and identification include stolen mail, pencils, pens, typewriters, check protectors, computer systems, photographic and printing equipment, blankets, enlargers and reducers, film, cameras, digital image cameras, computer scanners, background material for photographs, printing plates, photocopy machines, word processors and photo processing computer software programs, check making software such as Versa Check, items that can read, upload or download the contents of the magnetic strips found on credit and identification cards, stamps, seals, literature on printing and photography, silk screen equipment, inks and paints, photographs, plastic sheets, items for heating plastic sheets including irons and microwave ovens, plastic credit card blanks, drivers license blanks , trimmers, and laminators.

Any credit cards, checks, driver's licenses, or other identification not bearing the names of the parties found inside the location and any wallets, or purses containing such credit cards, checks, drivers licenses, or other identification.

Identity Theft – Computers, Credit Cards, Checks, and Identification-Affidavit

Based upon your Affiant's training, experience and conversations that your Affiant had with other Law Enforcement Officers and/or reports that your Affiant has read, your Affiant knows that credit and check fraud suspects often use computers as tools of their crime(s), such as making credit purchases over the Internet, and storing stolen credit card and check numbers. Suspect(s) engaged in the crimes of Identity Theft often use computers to manufacture and/or alter forged and/or counterfeit checks, identification cards, and/or Social Security cards for the purposes of committing credit and/or check fraud crimes. There are numerous items used to prepare and foster the forging of checks, credit cards, and identification cards that are list in this Search Warrant. Frequently names are located during the service of Search Warrant that does not belong to the suspect(s) that are Identity Theft in nature. These Names may be on computers, credit cards, checks, driver's licenses, identification cards and/or Social Security cards.

Business - Major -Fraud – ALL- Business –Records-Search Warrant

If an enterprise can be shown to be "permeated with fraud," then virtually all records can be seized even though not necessarily every record will be related to a fraudulent transaction.

Seizure of documents, business records, files, computers, and storage devices in the fraud business. The business is pervasively involved in cases of fraud, which causes the seizure of all business items.

Business - Major -Fraud – ALL- Business –Records-Affidavit

Based upon your Affiant's training, experience and conversations that your Affiant had with other Law Enforcement Officers and/or reports that your Affiant has read, yours Affiant knows that the business is permeated with fraud. Yours Affiant is seeking all documents relating to the suspected criminal area and will not remove any severable portions of the documents, which appear to relate to legitimate activities. (Place in a statement of the Basis for the Conclusion, It is not necessary that the Affidavit/Statement of Probable Cause supporting the Search Warrant set forth factual evidence demonstrating that every part of the enterprise is engaged in fraud) (Rather the Affidavit need contain only sufficient factual evidence of fraudulent activity, inferring that those activities are the tip of the iceberg)

Counterfeit US Currency-Search Warrant

Counterfeit United States currency in any denomination, green ink, black ink, red ink, cleaning solvents, printing presses, drying powders, photography equipment, color copying machines, toner, paper, counterfeit note aging paraphernalia, including, poker chips, marbles and other small items used to counterfeit notes; written articles on the manufacturing of counterfeit currency; computer hardware and software; articles of personal property tending to establish and document sales of counterfeit currency, consisting in part of and including, United States currency, gold, precious metals, jewelry and financial instruments, including stocks and bonds which are fruits, business records, buyer(s) lists, seller lists, address books and telephone lists, and other documentation related to the sale and transfer of counterfeit currency; and papers, documents and effects tending to show possession.

Counterfeit US Currency-Affidavit

Based upon your Affiant's training, experience and conversations that your Affiant had with other Law Enforcement Officers and/or reports that your Affiant has read, your Affiant knows that the counterfeiting of US Currency occurs in many different way and that many types of equipment are used during the counterfeiting. The counterfeit US Currency can be found in many states of the counterfeiting and that some counterfeit bills can be found just lying around the rooms where they are counterfeited. A lot of real US Currency can also be found at the sites because the counterfeiter get real money for their counterfeiting and trade counterfeit currency for real money. Seizure of counterfeit US Currency, counterfeiting equipment and real US Currency is necessary when service Search Warrants on counterfeit US Currency sites.

Telemarketing Fraud-Search Warrant

Any credit cards; credit card invoices or drafts, whether blank or filled in; merchant agreements; credit card account numbers in any form; customer lists; telephone records; items used to prepare credit card invoices or drafts, such as typewriters, typewriter ribbons, computer(s), word processors, word processor discs, pencils, pens, stamps; records of business activity involving credit card transactions, including journals, bank records, checks, charge summaries, merchant account contracts, or other records; credit card imprinters, merchant plates, merchant identification cards; contracts, tape recordings of telephone calls; and contracts with financial institutions, credit card holders, employees, or other merchants. Pitch sheets, scripts, tapes, or other training material in sales techniques that have been used during telemarketing.

Telemarketing Fraud-Affidavit

Based upon your Affiant's training, experience and conversations that your Affiant had with other Law Enforcement Officers and/or reports that your Affiant has read, your Affiant knows that suspects use Telemarketing to commit felony crimes. They use credit cards; credit card invoices or drafts, whether blank or filled in; merchant agreements; credit card account numbers in any form; customer lists; telephone records. They use numerous items to prepare credit card invoices or drafts. They use records of business activity involving credit card transactions frequently. They also use pitch sheets, scripts, tapes, or other training material in sales techniques that have been used during telemarketing.

Counterfeit Credit/Gift Cards-Search Warrant

Any items commonly used to manufacture, alter, counterfeit, prepare and/or foster the forging of credit cards, gift cards and identification; examples of such items include stolen mail, computer systems, media storage devices, CD rewriters, photographic and printing equipment, enlargers and reducers, film, cameras, digital image cameras, computer scanners, background material for photographs, word processors and photo processing computer software programs, items that can read, upload or download the contents of the magnetic strips found on credit and identification cards, stamps, seals, literature on printing and photography, silk screen equipment, inks and paints, photographs, plastic sheets, items for heating plastic sheets, plastic credit card blanks, drivers license blanks , and laminators.

Failure to Disclose Origin of Recordings - Video Piracy - 653w PC-Search Warrant

Relative to 653w of the California Penal Code (Failure to Disclose Origin of Recordings,) your Affiant request the following items to be seized from the owner, his agent, his manager or clerk on duty at the above location:

All copies of videocassettes made or used in violation of the copyright owner's exclusive rights.

Any documents, labels, VCR box covers or devices used in the support of making counterfeit copies of video cassettes and/or DVD's.

Any videocassette recorders, DVD recorders, devices, cables, monitors, electrical equipment or related gear used in the illegal duplication of videocassettes and/or DVD's.

Any documents tending to show order lists, inventories, exchange of moneys, or supplies of videocassettes and/or DVD's.

Failure to Disclose Origin of Recordings - Video Piracy - 653w PC-Affidavit

Based upon your Affiant's training, experience and conversations that your Affiant had with other Law Enforcement Officers and/or reports that your Affiant has read, your Affiant knows that business(es) can do video and digital image counterfeiting relative to 653w of the California Penal Code (Failure to Disclose Origin of Recordings), your Affiant requests that various video items are to be seized from the owner, his agent, his manager and/or clerk on duty at the above location(s).

Manufacture or Sale of Counterfeit Registered Mark - Trade Mark - 350 PC-Search Warrant

All unauthorized items such as (product name) products which reproduce, copy, counterfeit, imitate, replicate or bear counterfeit trademarks, trade names, logos or designs, such as, patches, watches, T-shirts, denims, caps, hardware or any other unauthorized items which imitate or bear unauthorized replications of the trademarks, names, logos or designs of items including but not limited to (product name).

Any sales, supplier and/or customer journals, ledgers, sales slips, invoices, purchase orders, inventory control documents, bank records, catalogs, recordings of any type whatsoever, client lists, telephone lists, telephone bills, cellular telephone bills, shipping documents, packaging materials, labels, records of shipments made by common carriers and all other business records and documents believed to concern the manufacture, distribution, importation, purchase, advertising, sale or offering for sale of the aforementioned infringing or unauthorized products.

Genuine products such as (product name) products/manufacturers when found in areas, locations or situations where it would suggest that these products were utilized in the design of counterfeit products or for comparison with the counterfeit product(s).

Any manufacturing equipment or means of production, such as any sewing machines, silk screen printing machines, T-shirt drying machines, silk screen, or other items which show a means of manufacture of counterfeit items, when found at the Search Warrant location.

Manufacture or Sale of Counterfeit Registered Mark - Trade Mark - 350 PC-Affidavit

Based upon your Affiant's training, experience and conversations that your Affiant had with other Law Enforcement Officers and/or reports that your Affiant has read, your Affiant knows that business(es) and/or individuals can have items that have counterfeit registered marks, Trade Marks per Penal Code Section 350. Your Affiant requests the seizure of item in this category; Any sales, supplier and/or customer journals, ledgers, sales slips, invoices, purchase orders, inventory control documents, bank records, catalogs, recordings of any type whatsoever, client lists, telephone lists, telephone bills, cellular telephone bills, shipping documents, packaging materials, labels, records of shipments made by common carriers and all other business records and documents believed to concern the manufacture, distribution, importation, purchase, advertising, sale or offering for sale of the aforementioned infringing or unauthorized products.

Genuine products/manufacturers when found in areas, locations or situations where it would suggest that these products were utilized in the design of counterfeit products or for comparison with the counterfeit product(s).

Any manufacturing equipment and/or means of production, such as any sewing machines, silk screen printing machines, T-shirt drying machines, silk screen, or other items which show a means of manufacture of counterfeit items, when found at the Search Warrant location.

Software Trademark Counterfeiting-Search Warrant

Any and All computer related items or documents containing the word "Microsoft" or "Windows", or containing known "Microsoft" product logo's; such as; labels, diskettes, CD-R's, CD-RW's, DVD's, envelopes, packaging materials, boxes, license agreements, holograms, certificates of authenticity, registration material, and instruction manuals.

Any and all equipment related to the production of counterfeit materials, such as; any computers, diskette copy machines, CD-Rom and DVD duplication equipment, shrink wrapping equipment, printing equipment, labeling equipment, and manufacturing supplies such as diskettes, CD-R's, CD-RW's, DVD's and CD-Rom cases, blank labels, plastic shrink wrap material, envelopes, and printing supplies.

Cash, checks, financial instruments, and other items of value that may be taken in exchange for the counterfeit merchandise.

Any financial documentation for the business "(suspect company name)", "(suspect's name)", whether in paper form or stored on computer media; such as, personal income tax records, business records, banking records, and sales, order or purchase records, and receipts.

All items, which may tend to identify other members of this on-going criminal enterprise, whether in paper form or stored on computer media; such as; phone bills, phone records, business cards, and books.

Indicia: items which show or tend to show persons and property connected to the location being searched, or subjects contacted at, working, or residing at, the location being searched.

Software Counterfeiting-Search Warrant

Any and all records, such as, invoices, checks, purchase orders, receipts, and bills of sale pertaining to the purchase and/or sale of any software product(s), whether stored on paper, on electronically readable or magnetic media such as tape, cassette, disk, diskette, or on memory storage devices such as optical disks, programmable instruments such as telephones, personal data assistants, electronic address books, calculators, or any other storage media, together with indicia of use, ownership, possession, or control of such records;

Any copies of software, supporting manuals, documents, certificates of authenticity and/or packing that contains a counterfeit mark at the time this Search Warrant is served;

Material commonly used on or in connection with the production, packaging and distribution of counterfeit software such as, labels, stickers, boxes, holograms, certificates of authenticity, adhesive label certificates of authenticity, cartons, labeled and unlabeled compact disks, instruction manuals, whether intact or in the form of individual pages, "glass masters" and "metal stampers";

Any packaging material used on or in connection with suspected "bundling" of the counterfeit trademark software including shrink wrap machines, rolls of plastic wrap, heat guns, CD jewel cases, blank CDs, master CDs, colored inks, foil, silk screening supplies, photograph supplies, software slip covers and key code labels;

Machines commonly used as the means of production, sale, distribution or manufacture of counterfeit software such as, disk copy machines, silk screening machines, printing presses, embossers, wrapping machines, photography equipment, foil machines, hologram makers, computers, and/or printers;

Records related to the production, sale, distribution or manufacture of counterfeit software such as, records of sales, orders, purchases, storage, shipments, and payments for counterfeit software;

Records related to the purchase or acquisition of materials and equipment intended for as the means of production, sale, distribution, or manufacture of counterfeit software including printing supplies and equipment, packaging supplies and equipment, shipping supplies and equipment, manufacturing supplies and equipment, to include invoices, orders, packing slips, bills of lading, shipment receipts, bills, account statements, and correspondence;

Employee personnel records which show the names, addresses, telephone numbers, positions held and job responsibilities of current and past employees at the location where this Search Warrant is beings served and/or (Company Name), who may have participated in or witnessed the production and/or sale(s) of counterfeit software;

Banking, business and financial records reflecting the location, distribution and flow of proceeds from the illegal production, sale, distribution, and manufacture of counterfeit software, including financial account information, account applications, account statements, account registers, locations of safe deposit records, sales tax records, income tax records, payroll records, payroll tax records, wire transfer receipts, deposit slips, cancelled checks, money orders, cashier checks, bank statements, cash, correspondence, records that tend to show wire transfers or other movement of funds obtained in the trafficking of counterfeit software. Records that tend to show the movement and expenditure of funds for the purpose of concealing their true source or for the purpose of "laundering" illegally obtained proceeds of criminal activity, documentation-showing control of ownership of safety deposit boxes.

Software Trademark Counterfeiting-Affidavit

Based upon your Affiant's training, experience and conversations that your Affiant had with other Law Enforcement Officers and/or reports that your Affiant has read, your Affiant knows that computer software can be "trademark" counterfeited. That any computer related items or documents containing the word "Microsoft" or "Windows", or containing known "Microsoft" product logo's; such as; labels, diskettes, CD-R's, CD-RW's, DVD's, envelopes, packaging materials, boxes, license agreements, holograms, certificates of authenticity, registration material, and instruction manuals should will be at the location(s) listed on this Search Warrant. All items should be seized as evidence.

Your Affiant wants all cash, checks, financial instruments, and other items of value that may be taken in exchange for the counterfeit merchandise. Any financial documentation for the business "(suspect company name)", "(suspect's name)", whether in paper form or stored on computer media; such as, personal income tax records, business records, banking records, and sales, order or purchase records, and receipts.

Your Affiant requests all items, which may tend to identify other members of this on-going criminal enterprise, whether in paper form or stored on computer media; such as; phone bills, phone records, business cards, and books. Indicia: items which show or tend to show persons and property connected to the location being searched, or subjects contacted at, working, and/or residing at, the location being searched.

Software Counterfeiting

Based upon your Affiant's training, experience and conversations that your Affiant had with other Law Enforcement Officers and/or reports that your Affiant has read, your Affiant knows that computer software can be counterfeited. At the location of the Search Warrant items of counterfeit software are to be seized. Records, such as, invoices, checks, purchase orders, receipts, and bills of sale pertaining to the purchase and/or sale of any software product(s) can be found at the location. Programmable instruments such as telephones, personal data assistants, electronic address books, calculators, or any other storage media, together with show the of use, ownership, possession, or control of such records.

Frequently there are copies of software, supporting manuals, documents, certificates of authenticity and/or packing that contain counterfeit marks at the time this Search Warrant is served. Material commonly used on or in connection with the production, packaging and distribution of counterfeit software. Any packaging material used on or in connection with suspected "bundling" of the counterfeit trademark software. Machines commonly used as the means of production, sale, distribution or manufacture of counterfeit software. Records related to the production, sale, distribution or manufacture of the counterfeit software. Records related to the purchase or acquisition of materials and equipment intended for as the means of production, sale, distribution, or manufacture of counterfeit software.

Employee personnel records which show the names, addresses, telephone numbers, positions held and job responsibilities of current and past employees at the location where this Search Warrant is beings served, who may have participated in or witnessed the production and/or sale(s) of counterfeit software.

Banking, business and financial records reflecting the location, distribution and flow of proceeds from the illegal production, sale, distribution, and manufacture of counterfeit software. Records that tend to show wire transfers or other movement of funds obtained in the trafficking of counterfeit software need to be seized. Records that tend to show the movement and expenditure of funds for the purpose of concealing their true source or for the purpose of "laundering" illegally obtained proceeds of criminal activity and documentation showing control of ownership of safety deposit boxes all may be found at the location

Audio Recording / Counterfeiting - (RIAA) -Search Warrant

All analog or digital audio recording(s) in audio or video cassette(s), vinyl album or compact disk (CD) format; partially or fully assembled and packaged, which are blank or stamped, or affixed with counterfeit labels, trademarks, and/or stating a false origin of manufacturer, or failing to disclose the true origin of any manufacturer, and whether or not loaded with recording tape. Audio or video tapes, vinyl disks or CD's used as master recordings, unstamped parts including cassette cartridges, vinyl disks and CD's, and printed paper products such as insert cards or inlay cards; cartridge labels, plastic/cellophane wrapping, and equipment utilized to produce finished illicit audio and video recordings to include, such as, tape loaders, audio and video duplicators, paper printing or duplicating equipment, printing plates, printing plate developing machines and associated raw product, on-cartridge printing machines, spools of magnetic tape, plastic library boxes and/or jewel boxes, and all related business records such as, catalogs, ledgers, number systems, order sheet, invoices, shipping records, customer lists, address books, telephone diaries and toll records, bank account records, state and federal income and property tax records.

Audio Recording Counterfeiting - (RIAA)-Affidavit

Based upon your Affiant's training, experience and conversations that your Affiant had with other Law Enforcement Officers and/or reports that your Affiant has read, your Affiant knows that audio recording can be counterfeited and that those items are at the location of this Search Warrant. The seizure of the counterfeit audio recording and the manufacturing equipment needs to be from this location during the service of this Search Warrant. Also all related business records such as, catalogs, ledgers, number systems, order sheet, invoices, shipping records, customer lists, address books, telephone diaries and toll records, bank account records, state and federal income and property tax records need to be seized.

Civilian Experts to Assist at the Search Warrant Site(s) - (RIAA)- Search Warrant

The court authorizes the use of employee(s) of the Recording Industry Association of America, Inc. (R.I.A.A.) to accompany the Peace Officers during the execution of this Search Warrant for the purpose of assisting in the identification of piratical sound recordings and/or their components as provided for under California Penal Code section 1530. Expert assistance is needed in the identification of counterfeit, pirated and/or bootlegged sound recordings and/or their components.

Civilian Experts to Assist at the Search Warrant Site(s) – (RIAA)-Affidavit

Based upon your Affiant's training, experience and conversations that your Affiant had with other Law Enforcement Officers and/or reports that your Affiant has read, your Affiant wants the court to authorize the use of an employee(s) of the Recording Industry Association of America, Inc. (R.I.A.A.) to accompany the Peace Officers during the execution of this Search Warrant for the purpose of assisting in the identification of piratical sound recordings and/or their components as provided for under California Penal Code section 1530. Expert assistance is needed in the identification of counterfeit, pirated and/or bootlegged sound recordings and/or their components.

Substitute Custodian of Evidence – Booking Away from Agency - (RIAA) -Search Warrant

IT IS HEREBY ORDERED, that the Recording Industry Association of America (RIAA) serve as the Substitute Custodian of Evidence that is seized pursuant to this Search Warrant at the specific request of the River City Police Department. The evidence / items seized during this Search Warrant shall remain available to the River City Police Department and the court of jurisdiction for whatever reason deemed necessary by said agency or court and remains bound by further orders of this court or court of jurisdiction.

All items seized pursuant to this Search Warrant shall be placed in a secure storage area, at a bonded warehouse approved by the River City Police Department. At the time of seizure and upon proper inventory of said seized items, exemplars may be removed and/or given for examination to representatives of member companies for authentication purposes. The exemplars will be returned to the evidence storage location when no longer needed for authentication, court, and prosecution and/or defense purposes.

Substitute Custodian of Evidence - Booking Away From Agency - (RIAA)-Affidavit

Based upon your Affiant's training, experience and conversations that your Affiant had with other Law Enforcement Officers and/or reports that your Affiant has read, your Affiant knows that there is a large quantity of merchandise normally seized in these cases and the burden it places on the River City Police Department's Property Detail. Your Affiant wants the Recording Industry Association of America (RIAA) to serve as the Substitute Custodian of Evidence for property that is seized pursuant to this Search Warrant. The evidence / items seized during this Search Warrant shall remain available to the River City Police Department and the court of jurisdiction for whatever reason deemed necessary by said agency or court and remains bound by further orders of this court or court of jurisdiction.

All items seized pursuant to this Search Warrant shall be placed in a secure storage area, at a bonded warehouse approved by the River City Police Department. At the time of seizure and upon proper inventory of said seized items, exemplars may be removed and/or given for examination to representatives of member companies for authentication purposes. The exemplars will be returned to the evidence storage location when no longer needed for authentication, court, and prosecution and/or defense purposes.

The Search Warrant: Narcotics and Gangs

Narcotic - General-Search Warrant

The description should specify the type of controlled substance to be seized, such as heroin, cocaine, marijuana, methamphetamine, etc. The use of the generic terms "controlled substances," "narcotics," or "dangerous drugs," without further description might be held by a reviewing court to be too vague.

The description of items to be seized should also include paraphernalia commonly associated with the sale, storage, possession, and use of the controlled substance.

. . . heroin and paraphernalia related to the use and sale of heroin, including hypodermic syringes, hypodermic needles, eye droppers, spoons, cotton, milk sugar, scales and other weighing devices, balloons, condoms, paper bindles, and measuring devices.

The affidavit may contain the opinion of a narcotics expert (usually the affiant) that paraphernalia will be found on the premises. Case law has held that where drugs are possessed for use or sale, it is reasonable to infer that paraphernalia for their use or sale will also be present

Ledger buyer lists, sellers' lists and recordations of distribution and sales of drugs may also be seized.

The warrant should include the seizure of articles that tend to identify the persons in control of the controlled substances and paraphernalia seized.

For example:

. . . articles of property tending to establish the identity of persons in control of premises, vehicles, storage areas, and containers being searched, including computers and the electronic files contained within, utility company receipts, rent receipts, addressed envelopes, and keys.

Narcotics – General-Affidavit

Based upon your Affiant's training, experience and conversations that your Affiant had with other Law Enforcement Officers and/or reports that your Affiant has read, your Affiant knows that the trafficking of large quantities of controlled substances requires the cooperation and association of numerous individuals. As a result, persons who traffic in narcotics will often possess documents that will identify other members of the organization such as telephone book(s), address book(s), telephone bill(s), and other paperwork documenting the name(s), address(es) and telephone numbers of co-conspirators. It is also your Affiant's experience that co-conspirators will retain address(s) and telephone numbers of other co-conspirators in the same way that a business will maintain records.

Your Affiant knows that narcotics, dangerous drugs, amphetamine / methamphetamine, cocaine, heroin, marijuana, and paraphernalia related to the use and/or sale of such substances can be found at Search Warrant sites and that firearms and other weapons, as well as large sums of cash are frequently found during the service of Search Warrants.

Narcotic - Amphetamine / Methamphetamine-Search Warrant

Methamphetamine and methamphetamine paraphernalia, consisting by way of example, scales and other weighing devices, paper bindles, tin foil, plastic baggies and glass vials, measuring devices and containers commonly associated with the storage and use of methamphetamine; and articles of personal property tending to establish and document sales of methamphetamine, consisting in part of and including U.S. currency, buyer lists, seller lists and recordations of sales; and articles of personal property tending to establish the existence of a conspiracy to sell methamphetamine, consisting in part of and including personal telephone books, address books and telephone bills. Articles of personal property tending to establish the identity of persons in control of premises, vehicles, storage areas or containers where methamphetamine may be found consisting in part of and including utility company receipts cancelled mail envelopes and keys, purchase receipts, tax statements and photographs.

Narcotic - Amphetamine / Methamphetamine Dealer-Search Warrant

Methamphetamine; paraphernalia commonly associated with the packaging, storage, sale, and use of methamphetamine, including scales, weighing devices, and measuring devices, packaging materials including paper bindles, glass vials, and plastic baggies, foils, sifters, filters, screens and cutting agents; articles of personal property tending to establish and document sales of methamphetamine including U.S. currency, foreign currency, negotiable instruments, buyers lists, seller lists, and recordations of sales, however recorded or memorialized; articles of personal property tending to establish the existence of a conspiracy to sell methamphetamine, including personal telephone books, ledgers, address books, telephone bills, and other papers and documents containing lists of names, however recorded or memorialized; articles of personal property tending to establish the identity of persons in control of premises, vehicles, storage areas and containers being searched, including computers and the electronic files contained within, utility company receipts, rent receipts, addressed envelopes, photographs, and keys.

Narcotic - Cocaine-Search Warrant

Cocaine (described as a white, crystalline powdery substance); base form of Cocaine (Rock Cocaine); paraphernalia commonly associated with the possession, packaging and/or sale of Cocaine such as scales, weighing devices and measuring devices, packaging materials including paper bindles, glass vials and plastic baggies, foil, sifters, filters, screens and cutting agents, recordation of the purchase and/or sales of Cocaine including ledgers, notebooks, pay/owe sheets, personal phone books, and/or personal photographs which document possession, sales and/or possession for sale of Cocaine, firearms and other weapons, as well as large sums of cash.

Narcotic – Cocaine Dealer-Search Warrant

. . . cocaine; narcotic paraphernalia, including scales and other weighing devices, measuring devices, and containers of various types commonly associated with the sale and possession of cocaine, including paper bindles, glass vials, plastic baggies, foils, sifters, filters, screens, and cutting agents; articles of personal property tending to establish and document sales of cocaine, including U.S. currency, buyer lists, seller lists, and recordations of sales; articles of personal property tending to establish the existence of a conspiracy to sell cocaine, including personal telephone books, address books, telephone bills, papers and documents containing lists of names; and articles of personal property tending to establish the identity of persons in control of the premises, vehicles, storage areas, and containers being searched, including computers and the electronic files contained within, utility company receipts, rent receipts, addressed envelopes and keys.

Narcotic-Heroin-Search Warrant

Heroin; paraphernalia commonly associated with the possession, packaging, and/or sale of Heroin such as hypodermic needles, hypodermic syringes, eyedroppers, spoons, cotton, dilatants, blenders, sifters, filters, scales, weighing devices, measuring devices, balloons, condoms, paper bindles, plastic baggies and cellophane, recordation of the purchase and/or sales of Heroin, including ledgers, notebooks, pay/owe sheets, personal phone books, and/or personal photographs which document possession, sales and/or possession for sale of Heroin, firearms and other weapons, as well as large sums of cash.

Narcotic - Heroin Dealer-Search Warrant

. . . heroin; paraphernalia related to the use and sale of heroin, including hypodermic needles, hypodermic syringes, eye droppers, spoons, cotton, milk sugar, scales and other weighing devices, balloons, condoms, paper bindles, measuring devices; articles tending to establish and document sales of heroin, including U.S. currency, buyer lists, seller lists, and recordations of sales; articles of personal property tending to establish the existence of a conspiracy to sell heroin, including personal telephone books, address books, telephone bills, papers and documents containing lists of names; and articles of personal property tending to establish the identity of persons in control of the premises, vehicles, storage areas, and containers being searched including computers and the electronic files contained within, utility company receipts, rent receipts, addressed envelopes, and keys.

Narcotic - Marijuana-Search Warrant

. . . marijuana; paraphernalia commonly associated with the storage and use of marijuana, including pipes, sifters, alligator clips, baggies, scales and other weighing devices; and articles of personal property tending to establish the identity of persons in control of the premises, vehicles, storage areas, and containers being searched, including computers and the electronic files contained within, utility company receipts, rent receipts, addressed envelopes, and keys.

Also, property or items utilized for the cultivation of marijuana, such as seeds, fertilizer, irrigation devices, garden tools, growing containers, electrical devices which aid in the growth of marijuana plants, such as timers, pumps, ballast, lights, climate control devices, generators, and books or instructional manuals to aid in the growing of marijuana, firearms and other weapons, as well as large sums of cash.

Narcotic – Marijuana Cultivation-Search Warrant

Marijuana and paraphernalia commonly associated with the growing, processing, storage and use of marijuana, consisting in part and including but not limited to, pipes, sifters, alligator clips, baggies, scales and other weighing devices, also articles of personal property tending to show the identity of persons in control of premises, vehicles, storage areas, or containers where marijuana may be found. In terms of outdoor cultivation, including but not limited to pipes (buried or above ground), hoses or other forms of irrigation systems consistent with marijuana cultivation; other trees, shrubs or plants planted or maintained in a manner to hide the marijuana plants being tended from ground or aerial view; shovels and hoes and other implements consistent with cultivation; plant fertilizer, seeds, sheds/facilities arranged for purposes of hanging, drying, processing and packaging of marijuana for distribution, and security devices or systems including but not limited to video surveillance, booby traps and armed security personnel or devices. In terms of indoor cultivation, including but not limited to, indoor grow lights, tubing or hoses or pipes arranged for use as an irrigation system for watering individuals plants or maintaining a hydroponic garden, seeds, plant medium, various sizes of pots, foil to cover walls or ceilings to reflect light/heat inward (improving growth patterns and/or limiting heat escape), transformers, heating and cooling and lighting systems for cultivation, security systems including but not limited to video surveillance, booby traps and armed security personnel or devices, facilities for hanging, drying, processing, storing, packaging and mailing of marijuana for distribution. Also, literature, magazines and computer data re cultivation techniques, especially those articles and documents specifically related to marijuana.

Also, paperwork and documentation, including but not limited to utility receipts, rent receipts, addressed mail, photographs and any currency and coins to show monies used in narcotics transactions, pays and owes regarding distribution and materials for packaging and mailing quantities of narcotics.

Any and all computer equipment or other electronic storage devices capable of storing electronic data regarding above items, including magnetic tapes, floppy disks, hard drive, viewing screens, disk or tape drives, central processing units, printers, and all software necessary to retrieve electronic data, including operating systems, database, spreadsheet, word processing and graphics programs, all manuals for operation of computer and software together with all handwritten notes or printed confidential password lists to enter secured files. Also any print outs throughout location or trash re above items, and indication of Internet usage and "favorite" or "bookmark" Internet locations relevant to use, cultivation and trafficking of marijuana and other narcotics.

Narcotic – Clandestine Laboratory-Search Warrant

Methamphetamine and precursors and derivatives of same; chemicals used in the manufacture of methamphetamine, including by way of example:

Acetic Anhydride, Acetic Acid, Acetone, Aluminum Foil, Amphetamine, Chloroform, Ephedrine, Norephedrine, or Pseudoephedrine, Ethanol, Ethyl Ether, Formamide, Freon, Hydriodic Acid, Hydrochloric Acid, Hydrogen Gas, Hydrogen Chloride Gas, Iodine, Isopropanol, Lithium Aluminum Hydride, Mercuric Chloride, Methanol, Methylamine, Palladium Black, Phenyl-2-Propanone (P2P), Phenylacetic Acid (PAA), Phosphorus Pentachloride, Platinum, Potassium Hydroxide, Red Phosphorus, Sodium Sulfate, Sodium Acetate, Sodium Thiosulfate, Sodium Hydroxide, Sodium Chloride, Sulfuric Acid, Thionyl Chloride, Round Bottom Flasks, Condensers, Heating Mantles, Tubing, Circulating Pumps, Separatory Funnels, Beakers, Vacuum Flasks, Vacuum Pumps, PH Paper, PH Meters, Thermometers, Transformers, Hydrogenators, Funnels, Chemical Formulas, Documents identifying co-conspirators, Documents showing ownership of vehicles, Documents identifying past or present clandestine laboratories, Documents showing storage areas for chemicals and laboratory equipment, Chemical company receipts, Records of drug transactions, Paperwork showing control of the lab site, premises, and storage lockers, keys and locks showing control and access to lab site premises or storage lockers.

Any unlabeled containers of liquids or dry chemicals; or liquids or dry chemicals that appear to be different than labeled.

Scales and balances

Evidence of conspiracy including books, ledgers, accounts payable and receivable, buy- owe sheets, contracts, letters and memoranda of agreement between the conspirators, formulas, receipts, telephone records, phone books, address books and other personal property tending to establish a conspiracy.

Financial records including expenses incurred in obtaining chemicals and apparatus and income derived from sales of finished product, as well as records showing legitimate income or the lack thereof and general living expenses.

Items or articles of personal property tending to show the identity of person(s) in ownership, or person(s) exercising dominion and control of said premises and/or vehicle(s) including rent receipts, telephone bills, utility receipts, telephone/address books, canceled mail, vehicle registration(s), keys, and photographs.

Narcotic – Clandestine Laboratory-Affidavit

Based upon your Affiant's training, experience and conversations that your Affiant had with other Law Enforcement Officers and/or reports that your Affiant has read, your Affiant knows that narcotic labs are used frequently in the manufacture of Amphetamine / Methamphetamine. These labs contain numerous items and chemicals for the manufacture, packaging, sale and possession of the narcotics. Documents, financial records, chemical recipes and formulas and/or other documents describing the manufacture of the narcotics, photographs, firearms and other weapons and large sums of cash can frequently be found at the Search Warrant location.

Narcotic – GHB Gamma Hydroxy Butyrate-Search Warrant

GAMMA HYDROXY BUTYRATE (GHB aka Scoop, G, Liquid X, Liquid Ecstasy, Easy Lay, Great Hormones at Bedtime, Salt Water, Water, Sodium Oxbate or Oxybutyrate, Grievous Bodily Harm, Female Viagra, Georgia Home Boy, Everclear, Aminos); any active analog of GHB, including but not limited to 1,4 Butanediol (aka, tetramethylene glycol or Sucol B), Gamma Butyl Lactone (an analog and precursor, with an aka of 2(3H) furanone di-hydroxy); Sodium 4-hydroxyvalerate (aka, GHV or 4-Methyl GHB or valeric acid) and narcotics paraphernalia consisting in part of, including but not limited to:

Any container capable of holding a liquid, such as water bottles, sports drink bottles (Gatorade or other brands), mouthwash bottles (large or sample size), vitamin and other pills bottles, spice bottles (clear or brown glass, such as vanilla or almond extract or food coloring), eyedroppers, medicinal style bottles with eyedropper in lid; child's bubble container, hair spray bottle (large or purse size), gallon jugs of auto window wash solution or any cleaning agent bottle, liquid eyewash or breath mint containers, any container marked GHB, whether liquid or powder, or marked Biosul or Borametz (or other name with ingredients listed as Russian pine needle oil extract) or marked Renewtrient, Blue Nitro, Revivarant, Regenergize, Firewater, Invigorate, Eclipse, G3, Gamma G, GHG or GHGold, Reactive, Rest-eze or Remforce (which may list the ingredient 2(3H)furanone di-hydroxy or di-hydro). The analog 1,4 butanediol may be listed as tetramethylene glycol or Sucol B on products with names such as Enliven, Serenity, Revitalize Plus, Thunder Nectar, Weight Belt Cleanser, Amino Flex, Jolt, Verve, Rejoov, Dream On, BVM, GHRE, NRG3, Promusol, etc.

While GHB is most commonly encountered in liquid form (in original form will be clear and only slightly thicker than water, but may be diluted or mixed with other drinks or colored for concealment), it may also be found in powdered form (it is hydroscopic and thus, if not well sealed, may turn into a mushy or putty form) and may be found as a powder in capsule form. Therefore, search to also include container which would be capable of holding a powder or pills, such as glass or plastic containers with screw on or snap on lids (such as butter containers, cosmetic cream containers, etc.), ziplock baggies; medical type containers for storage and dispensing of liquids (vials or injectable fluid types, possibly labeled "For research only"); or other containers associated with the storage and use of GHB. Also to be searched, refrigerators and freezers for containers of liquid, ice cube trays, blocks or other frozen containers of GHB or its analogs.

Any container of GHB precursor Gamma Butyl Lactone (size may vary from a few ounces to 55 gallon drum), sodium hydroxide or lye, baking soda (may be used in lieu of sodium hydroxy or lye), vinegar, muriatic acid, acetone (re powdered GHB or attempt to convert to powder), heating element (optional), multiple empty containers such as listed above for use in distribution. Also U.S. currency and any papers and documents tending to show possession for sale, such as lists of names or addresses or pay and owe records, buyers, sellers, manufacturers, chemical supply houses, order forms or receipts for purchase from chemical supply houses of above ingredients, shipping records, bills of lading, recipes, any bodybuilding magazine articles re GHB use, other magazine or computer articles re GHB use and manufacturing.

Narcotic – Ketamine-Search Warrant

KETAMINE (Ketamine Hydrochloride (hcl), aka Special K, K, Vitamin K, Chemical Virtual Reality, Psychedelic Heroin) an animal tranquilizer (behavioral analog of PCP) also used in human surgical procedures, any medical bottle marked Ketamine, Ketalar, Vetalar, Ketaset or with label removed containing a clear liquid (slightly thicker than water in appearance), box or label or product information sheet regarding Ketamine, any syringe containing a clear liquid or empty which may have been used and may contain residue or any white powdered substance on plate or other surface or in ziplock baggie or other container commonly associated with transporting powdered drugs, any plate, oven pan, microwave dish or interior of microwave or oven which may contain residue of Ketamine being dried upon or in that item. Any computer or other articles re Ketamine use and abuse; any packaging material with evidence of shipment from veterinary or other medical supply location. Small amber bottles or tiny "coke" spoons, straws, rolled papers or monetary bills used for snorting powdered substances.

Narcotic – LSD Lysergic Acid Diethylamide-Search Warrant

Lysergic Acid Diethylamide (LSD), which may be in the form of liquid, blotter paper dosages, on sugar cubes, in gel capsules or gel tab form, equipment, packaging and other paraphernalia commonly associated with LSD, including but not limited to eye droppers, capillary tubes, distilled water, alcohol (including Everclear alcohol), glass pans, weighing devices, perforating wheels (such as Dritz perforating wheel used in dressmaking) and perforating rulers, printing equipment, stamps with various designs and stamp ink pads, tin foil, cooling devices (such as refrigeration, ice chests, cool bags), water stained paper (including spiral notebooks--exhibiting indications of splashing on pages), printed blotter paper, tweezers or forceps, rubber gloves, various size containers for storage and transportation of liquid LSD (such as Visine or other eye wash bottles or Binanca Blast or Crystal Ice or other breath mint product containers), gelatin substances, food coloring, chemicals associated with the manufacturing of LSD, including but not limited to, acetonitrile (ether-like odor), diethylemine (DMT analog), ergotamine tartrate (E.T.), hydrazine (colorless, oily liquid with ammonia-like odor), hydrazine hydrate, lysergic acid, sulfur trioxide, trifluoro acetic anhydride, hydrochloric acid, sodium nitrite, sodium bicarbonate, and ether; all laboratory equipment and apparatus used in the manufacturing process, including three-necked round bottom flasks, condensing columns and other glassware, hoses, filter paper, heating mantel, pots, clamps, tubes, buckets, funnels, stirring sticks or rods, strainers, gloves and chemical containers; all paraphernalia used to package, store and distribute LSD, including, measuring and weighing devises, diluting agents, plastic bags and baggies, tinfoil, cellophane, perforated sheets of plastic used as diffusing light covers (LSD gel is sometimes dropped onto each perforated segment), blister pack "tops" (LSD gel dropped onto each segment) and other containers; all written or printed chemical formulas or books and papers containing chemical formulas for controlled substances; computer bookmarks and printouts or other computer documents regarding making, using or selling LSD, and all articles of personal property tending to establish the identity of the person or persons having possession of or dominion and control over said premises, vehicles, storage areas and containers where LSD, and the chemicals used to manufacture LSD or other narcotics and dangerous drugs and formulas are found, including rent receipts, utility receipts, opened mail envelopes, canceled checks, keys, buyer and seller lists and documentation of narcotics transactions.

Narcotic – PCP (Phencyclidine) -Search Warrant

PHENCYCLIDINE (PCP), a controlled substance; 1-piperidinocyclohexane carbonitrile (PCC), a controlled substance; all chemicals and raw materials and their containers used in the manufacture of phencyclidine or any of its analogs, including piperidine, cyclohexanone, bromobenzene, pyrolidine, morphaline, magnesium, sodium bisulfite, sodium cyanide, iodine crystals, ether (ethyl and petroleum), hydrochloric acid and lye, along with other chemicals consistent with the manufacture of phencyclidine; all laboratory equipment and apparatus used in the manufacturing process, including glassware, hoses, pots, clamps, tubes, buckets, trash cans, stirring sticks or rods, strainers, gloves and chemical containers; all paraphernalia used to package, store and distribute phencyclidine, including, measuring and weighing devises, diluting agents, plastic bags and baggies, tinfoil, cellophane and other containers; all written or printed chemical formulas or books and papers containing chemical formulas for controlled substances; and all articles of personal property tending to establish the identity of the person or persons having possession of or dominion and control over said premises, vehicles, storage areas and containers where phencylidine or PCC, and the chemicals used to manufacture phencyclidine or PCC or other narcotics and dangerous drugs and formulas are found, including rent receipts, utility receipts, opened mail envelopes, canceled checks, keys, buyer and seller lists and documentation of narcotics transactions

Narcotic – MDMA (3,4 Methylenedioxymethamphetamine) -
Search Warrant

MDMA (3,4 METHYLENEDIOXYMETHAMPHETAMINE) or analogs thereof (including but not limited to MDA, MDMB), also known as Ecstasy, X, XTC, E, Doves, Crowns, Jaw Breaker, Love Drug, Rolls, Street Rolls, D&G, DG, Mercedes, the Hug Drug, Smurfs,--a central nervous system stimulant/hallucinogen and a synthetic drug produced solely in clandestine laboratories. MDMA is found in either powder (white to tan or brown, but most commonly white or off-white) form or in pressed pill (any color) or capsule form. Pressed pills may have any logo or inscription or may be plain. Most common logos include a lightning bolt or dove or dollar sign imprint. The logo may be any animal or cartoon character or commercial logo such as Mitsubishi or Mercedes or Nike or letters such as D&G for the Italian clothing designers or JB for Jaw Breaker. A pill may be two-toned (white with blue or pink). Gel capsules may be full or only partially full and may be clear or any combination of colors. Gel caps in blue/white may be referred to as smurfs. Powder may be in a plastic ziplock baggie or any container that will hold a powder. Pills may be packaged with other pills of similar size and consistency or with candies of similar size and consistency. Wafer pills may be the size of a chewable vitamin C tab, even including dark specks in the white or off white pill.

Common indicators of MDMA use and distribution include packages of tootsie rolls (rolls are hand-heated to soften, an Ecstasy pill is pressed into the candy and it is then rewrapped—referred to as "Rolls"), bags of candy such as M&Ms or Skittles (pills floating among the candy in the bag), candy bead necklaces and bracelets (MDMA pills may be drilled and strung in with the candy beads), Vicks (or other brand) inhalers or surgical type face masks and bottles of Vicks (being on MDMA enhances the sensation felt from inhaling Vicks) and Tootsie Roll Pops or infant pacifiers (the Pops and pacifiers are used to reduce the grinding of teeth which is common while on MDMA) or personal vibrators or products such as Tiger Balm, used for massaging each other to help with the muscle spasms caused by MDMA use. While these items are not illegal, their presence along with other above items is indicative of use.

Steroids-Search Warrant

Anabolic Steroids, and related paraphernalia used for its ingestion and administration, including, but not limited to tablet splitters, hypodermic syringes, and hypodermic needles or varying gauges; items used for preparing Anabolic Steroids for street sales and/or storage, including plastic bags, foil blister packs, plastic canisters, small cardboard boxes and bubble wrap; articles of personal property tending to establish and document use and administration, sales, and transportation of Anabolic Steroids, consisting of buyer lists, seller lists, recordation of use and administration cycles and recordation of sales; articles of personal property tending to establish the existence of a conspiracy to use and administer, sell, and transport Anabolic Steroids, including personal telephone books, address books, telephone bills, papers and documents containing lists of names, addresses and phone numbers of Anabolic Steroids customers, and suppliers; articles of personal property tending to establish the identity of persons in control of the premises, vehicles, storage areas, and containers being searched including the utility company receipts, rent receipts, addressed envelopes, keys and photographs of the defendant(s) and their associates.

Anabolic steroids in either injectable or blister pack or bottle preparations such as: Abirol (methandienone), Adroyd (oxymetholone), Anabol (19-nortestosterone), Anaboleen (Androstanolone), Anabolex (Dihydrotestosterone), Anadrol-50 (oxymetholone), Anadroyd (oxymetholone), Anavar (oxandrolone), Androil Understor (testosterone undecanoate), Androfluorene (mesterolon), Androgenicum Prolangatum (Sustanon 250), Androin (methyltestosterone), Androlone (dihydrotestosterone), Androtardy 1 (testosterone enanthate), Androxan (andriosoxazole), Androxon (testosterone undecanoate), Bolasterone (dimethyltestosterone), Boldenone (boldenone undecylnate), Clostebol (chlorotestosterone), Danocrine (danazol), D-Bol (methandrostenelone), Deca-durabol (nandrolone decanoate), Deca-durabolin (nandrolone decanoate), Delastertryl (testosterone enanthate), Depo-testosterone (testosterone cypionate), Dianabol (methandrostenelone), Diandrone (dehydroisoandrosterone), Dostalon (dimethazine), Drolban (dromostanolone), Durabolin (nandrolone phenpropionate), Duraboral (ethylestrenol), Equibold (boldenone undecylnate), Equipoise (boldenone undecylnate), Ermaion (mestanolone), Finaject (parabolan acetate), Finajet (parabolan acetate), Fluotestin (fluoxymesterone), Gaebol (dehydromethyltestosterone), Genabol (norbolethone), Geno-cristaux (testosterone), Halostein (fluoxymesterone), Halotestin (fluoxymesterone), Hexahydrobenzyl (iontanyl), Hombreol (testosterone propionate), Kabolin (nandrolone decanoate), Malestrone (testosterone), Maxibolin (ethylestrenol), Mestoran (mesterolon), Mestoranum (mesterolon), metabolin (methandriol dipropionate), Metandren (methyltestosterone), Methalutin (methyl-19-nortestosterone), Methenolone Acetate (primobolan), Methenolone Enanthate (primobolan depot), Methosarb (calusterone), Myagen (dimethyltestosterone), Nabolin (dehydromethyltestosterone), Nandrolin (nandrolone phenpropionate), Nelevar (oxandrolone), Neo-ponden (Androisoxazole), Nerobil (dehydromethyltestosterone), Nibol (methenolone), Nilevar (norethandrolone), Nor-neutrormone (ethylnortestosterone), Orabolin (ethylestrenol), Oranabol (oxymestrone), Ora-testryl (fluoxymesterone), Oreton (testosterone propionate), Oreton Methyl (methyltestosterone), Orgabolin (ethylestrenol), Orgasteron (methyl-19-nortestosterone), Oxandrolone Spa (oxandrolone), Oxitosone(oxymetholone), Perandren (testosterone propionate), Primabolin (methenolone), Primobolin Acetate (primobolan), Primotest (testosterone), Pronabol (ethylnortestosterone), Proteina (dihydrotestosterone), Proviron (mesterolon), Psicosterone (dehydroepiandrosterone), Quad (testosterone propionate), Quindenione (parabolan), Restansol (testosterone undecanoate), Roxilon (dimethazine), Sanaboral (oxymestrone), Sostenon (sustanon 250), Steranabol (chlorotestosterone), Steranabol Depot (oxabolene), Sterandryl (testosterone propionate), Stromba (stanozolol), Teslac (testololactone), Testoenant (testosterone enanthate), Tevabolin (stanozolol), Theranabol (oxymestrone), Trenbolone (parabolan), Turinabol (cholortestosterone or dehydrochlormethyl-testosterone), Ultandren (fluoxymesterone), Winstrol (stanozolol), and Winstrol-V (stanozolol);

Plus other substances commonly abused by athletes in polydrug combination with anabolic steroids such as: APL (chorionic gonadrotropin), Ascellacrin (human growth hormone), Clomid or Omifin (fertility drug), Clomiphene (human chorionic gonadotropin), Crescormin (HGH), Cytomel SPA or Liothyronine (thyroid hormone), GH (growth hormone), Glucagon (hormone), HCG (human chorionic gonadotropin), HGH (human growth hormone), Humatrope (GH), Pregnyl (chorionic gonadotropin), Profasi (chorionic gonadotropin), Protropin (GH), Scmein (GH), STH or somatotrophic hormone (HGH), Thyroid (hormone), and Thyroxine (hormone);

Plus diuretics, anti-inflammatory medications, vitamins, stimulants, anti-estrogens, amino acids, neurotransmitters and tanning pills commonly utilized in conjunction with steroids, such as: Accutane (anti-acne), Aldactazide (diuretic), Bumex (diuretic), caffeine, cocaine, codeine, Cyproheptadine (weight promoter), Diazide or Dyazide (diuretic), Didrex (amphetamine), Eskatrol (amphetamine), Fastine (amphetamine), Feldene Cream, Gerobital, Guarana, Indocin (anti-inflammatory), L-Dopa or Levodopa (neurotransmitter), Lasix or Furosemide (diuretic), Minocin (antibiotic), Nolvadex or Tamoxifen Citrate (anti-estrogen), Octacosanol, Preludin or Phenmetrazine (amphetamine), Proteolytic enzymes (Papaine), Thiomucase, Trisoralen (tanning pill), Tryptophan; plus gamma hydroxy butyrate (GHB—which is commonly also abused by steroid users);

Plus, syringes, needles and other paraphernalia commonly associated with injecting and administering steroids, articles of personal property tending to establish and document sales of steroids, consisting in part of and including, U.S. currency, buyer lists, seller lists, and recordations of sales; calendars or date books or instructions re bodybuilding and weight training competitions with notations regarding typical steroid issues such as "cycling" (referring to periodic repetition of steroid abuse) or "stacking" (referring to simultaneous use of different anabolic steroids), notations regarding typical steroid street names such as A, BLAST, CYP, D-B, D-BALL OR D-BOL, DECA, DEPO, DUR, ENA, EQ, FIN, G, GROWTH, HOLTEST, MAXI, MT, PAR, PRIMO, PROP, SPA, STH, TC, TEST, V, W-V

Gang – Membership-Search Warrant

Any evidence of street gang membership, or affiliation with any street gang, such as any paraphernalia making any reference to the "Gang Name" street gang. Items such as any audio and/or video tapes making reference to the "Gang Name" street gang, and/or any drawings, miscellaneous writings, objects, and/or graffiti depicting gang members' names, initials, logos, monikers, slogans, and/or containing mention of street gang membership affiliation, activity, and/or identity, as it is your Affiant's experience that most street gang members are known by street names or monikers to their fellow gang members, and that they frequently write their names and/or monikers of their associates on walls, furniture, miscellaneous items or papers, both within and on their residences, and within and on their vehicles; any paintings, drawings, film (developed and undeveloped), photographs and/or photograph albums depicting persons, vehicles, weapons, and/or locations to be relevant on the question of gang membership or association, which depict items sought in this Search Warrant, and/or which depict evidence of any criminal activity;

Any newspaper clippings tending to relate details or reference to any crime or crimes of violence; any address books, lists of, or single references to, addresses or telephone numbers.

Any letters and/or documents, whether in actual written form or stored in an electronic manner, which make reference to membership and/or activities of any criminal street gang;

Gang – Membership-Affidavit

Based upon your Affiant's training, experience and conversations that your Affiant had with other Law Enforcement Officers and/or reports that your Affiant has read, it Affiant experience that most street gang members are known by street names or monikers to their fellow gang members, and that they frequently write their names or monikers of their associates on walls, furniture, miscellaneous items or papers, both within and on their residences, and within and on their vehicles; any paintings, drawings, film (developed and undeveloped), photographs or photograph albums depicting persons, vehicles, weapons, or locations which may appear upon observation to be relevant on the question of gang membership or association, or which may depict items sought and/or believed to be evidence in the case being investigated with this warrant, or which may depict evidence of any criminal activity, as it is your Affiant's experience that most gang members keep photographs and photograph albums in which are depicted: (1) fellow gang members who are posing and giving gang hand signs which indicate gang identity or affiliation; (2) gang members or associates posing with weapons, particularly firearms, which are often used for criminal activities; (3) gang members or associates posing beside vehicles which are occasionally used during the commission of crimes; and (4) gang members or associates posing at locations which are known to be specific gang hangouts; any newspaper clippings tending to relate details or reference to any crime or crimes of violence as it is your Affiant's experience that gang members maintain scrapbooks of newspaper articles which describe crimes committed by or against their gang; and any address books, list of, or single references to, addresses or telephone numbers of persons who may later be determined to belong to or be affiliated with any street gang/s, since it is your Affiant's experience that gang members frequently maintain the current phone numbers or addresses or fellow gang members with whom they associate.

Your Affiant requests permission to search for and seize any letters and/or documents, whether in actual written form or stored in an electronic (computerized) manner, which would appear to make reference to membership and/or activities of any criminal street gang. It is your Affiant's experience that gang members possess in their residences letters written by gang members to and from fellow gang members, relatives, girlfriends, boyfriends and friends. These letters contain current information about the activity of the gang and its members. They contain details of gang crimes by the individual gang members and criminal activity by the gang. They include information about gang membership, gang rosters, members and graffiti regarding the writer's gang. These letters are frequently directed to or received from gang members in-custody and they are intended to keep members apprised of what is going on with the gang and its enemies and allies.

It is also your Affiant's experience that gang members frequently possess compact disks (CDs) and digital video disks (DVDs) with gang graffiti and sometimes monikers on them. In addition, your Affiant has found that gang members frequently have video tapes and digital media files in their possession that depict gang activity such as gang members posing with and firing weapons, gang parties where gang members pose with weapons and flash gang signs with their hands, and make statements about their gang. These tend to show gang affiliation and may depict gang members with weapons used in crimes, and your Affiant requests permission to search for and seize any such items.

It is your Affiant's opinion that any evidence of gang membership or affiliation with any street gang is important as it may suggest motive for the commission of the crimes, as in this case, and it may provide evidence which tends to identify other persons who may have knowledge of or be involved in the commission of the crimes in the instant case, or it may tend to corroborate information given by other witnesses.

Gang - General Gang Information-Search Warrant

Any evidence of street gang membership or affiliation with any street gang, said paraphernalia such as reference to the "Gang Name". Any items such as any digital audio or video tapes or digital video images making reference to the "Gang Name" gang, or any blue or red rags; drawings or letters from or to Juvenile Hall, Jails, State Prisons, and/or Youth Authority Facilities, and/or objects of graffiti depicting gang members names, logos, initials, monikers, slogans, and/or containing mention of street gang membership, affiliation, activity, or identity;

Any written names or monikers on walls, furniture, miscellaneous items or papers, both within and on their residences, and/or within and on their vehicles; any paintings, drawings, film (developed and undeveloped), photographs and/or photograph albums depicting persons, vehicles, weapons, and/or locations;

Any photographs, digital images, videos, and photograph albums in which are depicted:

- Fellow gang members who are posing and giving gang hand signs, which indicate gang identity or affiliation;

- Gang members or associates posing with weapons, particularly firearms, which are often used for criminal activities;

- Gang members or associates posing beside vehicles, which are occasionally used during the commission of crimes;

- Gang members or associates posing at locations, which are known to be specific gang hangouts; any newspaper clippings tending to relate details or reference to any crime or crimes of violence;

- Any scrapbooks of newspaper articles, which describe crimes committed by and/or against their gang; any address books, list of, or single references to, addresses or telephone numbers of persons who may later be determined to belong to or be affiliated with any street gang/s;

- Any current phone numbers, addresses of fellow gang members with whom they associate;

•   Any letters and/or documents, whether in actual written form or stored in an electronic (computerized) manner, which would appear to make reference to membership and/or activities of any criminal street gang;

•   Any information about gang membership, gang rosters, members and/or graffiti regarding the writer's gang;

Any compact disks (CD) or digital video disks (DVDs) with gang graffiti and sometimes monikers on them, digital image files and video tapes which depict gang activity such as gang members posing with and firing weapons, gang parties where gang members pose with weapons and flash gang signs with their hands, and make statements about their gang;

The Search Warrant: Special Procedures

Federal Law Enforcement Officer(s) To Assist In Search Warrant-Search Warrant

Penal Code section 830.8 states that "Federal criminal investigators and law enforcement officers are not California peace officers . . ." However, they can be the affiant for a state-issued search warrant.

The court authorizes the use of Federal Agency personnel to accompany the Peace Officers executing this Search Warrant for the purpose of assisting in the service and execution of this Search Warrant as provided for under California Penal Code Section 1530 and 1538. The Federal Agency personnel can also assist in the computer examinations of the seized items.

Federal Law Enforcement Officer(s) To Assist In Search Warrant-Affidavit

Based upon your Affiant's training, experience and conversations that your Affiant had with other Law Enforcement Officers and/or reports that your Affiant has read, your Affiant requests that the court authorize the use of Federal Agency personnel to accompany the Peace Officers executing this Search Warrant for the purpose of assisting in the service and execution of this Search Warrant as provided for under California Penal Code Section 1530 and 1538. The Federal Agency personnel can also assist in the computer examinations of the seized items.

Civilian(s) To Assist At the Search Warrant Site(s)-Search Warrant

The court authorizes the use of person(s) who are not peace officers to accompany the Peace Officers during the execution this Search Warrant for the purpose of assisting in the service of this Search Warrant as provided for under California Penal Code Section 1530.

Civilian(s) To Assist At the Search Warrant Site(s)-Affidavit

Based upon your Affiant's training, experience and conversations that your Affiant had with other Law Enforcement Officers and/or reports that your Affiant has read, your Affiant wants the court to authorize the use of person(s) who are Not Peace Officers to accompany the Peace Officers during the execution of this Search Warrant for the purpose of assisting them in the service of this Search Warrant as provided for under California Penal Code Section 1530.

Special Master - Authorization-Search Warrant

Penal Code section 1525 states in part that the application for a search warrant shall specify when applicable, that the place to be searched is in the possession or under the control of an attorney, physician, psychotherapist, or clergyman.

Penal Code section 1524 subdivisions (c) through (f) provide that no search warrant shall issue for any documentary evidence in the possession or under the control of any person who is a lawyer, physician, psychotherapist or clergyman, and who is not reasonably suspected of criminal activity related to the documentary evidence, unless certain procedures involving a special master are followed. The statute provides for the appointment of a special master by the court, for procedures to be followed in the service of the warrant, and for a possible court hearing regarding any seized property. Any prosecutor or peace officer involved in the preparation of a search warrant that may require the appointment of a special master should carefully review this statute to ensure proper compliance with these procedures.

The special master procedures are limited to the four named professionals and do not extend to other professionals, such as experts and consultants, who might be hired by the named professionals.

The court authorizes the appointment of a Special Master pursuant to Penal Code section 1524, subdivision (d), to conduct the aforementioned search at the site listed on this Search Warrant. The Special Master shall accompany searching Peace Officers during the service of this Search Warrant. The Special Master shall seize any material that relates to a privilege, but is otherwise approved for seizure by this Search Warrant. The material shall be placed in a container and sealed, to be held and inspected by the Special Master, pending further order of the Special Master and / or the Court issuing this Search Warrant. If the data is in electronic form, the Special Master shall issue specific instructions for the search of the storage medium, in the Special Master's discretion. The cost of any Special Master shall be incurred by the Court, consistent with People v. Laff, (2001) 25 Cal.4th. 703, 737-744.

Special Master – Authorization-Affidavit

Based upon your Affiant's training, experience and conversations that your Affiant had with other Law Enforcement Officers and/or reports that your Affiant has read, your Affiant requests that the court authorize the appointment of a Special Master pursuant to Penal Code section 1524, subdivision (d), to conduct the aforementioned search at the site listed on this Search Warrant. The Special Master shall accompany searching Peace Officers during the service of this Search Warrant. The Special Master shall seize any material that relates to a privilege, but is otherwise approved for seizure by this Search Warrant. The material shall be placed in a container and sealed, to be held and inspected by the Special Master, pending further order of the Special Master and / or the Court issuing this Search Warrant. If the data is in electronic form, the Special Master shall issue specific instructions for the search of the storage medium, in the Special Master's discretion. The cost of any Special Master shall be incurred by the Court, consistent with People v. Laff, (2001) 25 Cal.4th. 703, 737-744.

Sealing "Statement of Probable Cause / Affidavit" – "Hobbs" - Search Warrant

In those cases in which the affidavit is based entirely upon the observations of the affiant, the credibility of the affiant as the source of information is established by the issuing magistrate accepting the affidavit. (*Skelton v. Superior Court* (1969) 1 Cal.3d 144, 154.) If the magistrate did not believe the affiant to be truthful in his statements, then the magistrate would not sign the affidavit and warrant. Also, all police officers are presumed to be credible for search warrant purposes. (*People v. Hill* (1974) 12 Cal.3d 731, 761.)

It is unusual for an affidavit to be based solely upon the observations of the affiant. Usually, other persons provide information to the affiant which is also included in the affidavit. For search warrant purposes, such persons are known as "informants."

Use of Informants -- Two-Prong Test

A valid search warrant may be issued based entirely upon information provided to the affiant by an informant. However, the basic requirements of factual sufficiency and reliability must be demonstrated.

This was set forth in general terms in *Aguilar v. Texas* (1964) 378 U.S. 108, 114 as follows:

Although an affidavit may be based on hearsay information and need not reflect the direct personal observations of the affiant, [citations], the magistrate must be informed of some of the underlying circumstances from which the informant concluded that the narcotics were where he claimed they were, and some of the underlying circumstances from which the officer concluded that the informant, whose identity need not be disclosed, [citations] was "credible" or his information "reliable".

Thus, the *Aguilar* case is often cited as establishing a "two-prong" test of the validity of a search warrant based solely upon an informant's statement. The two prongs require that:

 1) the underlying circumstances or factual basis of the informant's statement must be set forth -- thus, a mere statement by the informant that "Chris Bingham is dealing heroin" is insufficient -- and, 2) it must be shown that the informant was credible OR his information reliable.

Analysis of the two prongs shows that each actually has two parts. The first ("factual basis") prong requires that the informant's statement be: (a) factual, and (b) based upon personal knowledge.

(This will be discussed further in Section D.)

The second ("reliability") prong requires that the affidavit show that: (a) the informant himself is credible, or (b) that his information is reliable.

The informant himself may be shown to be credible either by showing that he comes within a category of persons all of whom are presumed credible, such as police officers or "citizen informants," or by showing that he has given accurate information on prior occasions and is thus a "tested informant." The informant's information may be shown to be reliable by corroborating it with other facts set forth in the affidavit. Either way, the magistrate is justified in relying upon the information provided by the informant.

IT IS HEREBY ORDERED, based upon a review of the Search Warrant Affidavit this court finds that there exists an overriding interest that overcomes the right of public access to the record; the overriding interest supports sealing the record; a substantial probability exists that the overriding interest will be prejudiced if the record is not sealed; the proposed sealing is narrowly tailored; an no less restrictive means exist to achieve the overriding interest.

Therefore it is ordered that the following portion of the Search Warrant Affidavit / Statement of Probable Cause identified as the "Confidential Attachment" be sealed and kept in the custody of the Affiant's law enforcement agency and not be made part of the public record until further order of this court or any competent court.

Sealing Statement of Probable Cause / Affidavit – Hobbs-Affidavit

Based upon your Affiant's training, experience and conversations that your Affiant had with other Law Enforcement Officers and/or reports that your Affiant has read, your Affiant requests that the following portion of the Search Warrant Affidavit / Statement of Probable Cause be ordered sealed by the Magistrate in order to implement the privilege under Evidence Code Sections 1040 to 1042 and to protect the identity of any confidential informant(s) and/or official information, pursuant to the Supreme Court decision in People v. Hobbs (1994) 7 Cal. 4th 948, and California Rule of Court Rule 243.1, subd. (d).

If any of the information within the requested sealed portion of the Affidavit / Statement of Probable Cause is made public, it will reveal or tend to reveal the identity of any confidential informant(s), imp-air further related investigations and endanger the life of the confidential informant(s).

Sealing Of Statement of Probable Cause / Affidavit - Child Pornography-Search Warrant

IT IS HEREBY ORDERED that the entire or designated portion of this Statement of Probable Cause / Affidavit used to support of this Search Warrant be sealed by court order until further order of this court.

This order is based upon the fact that designated material is significant that if possessed by non-law enforcement personnel would violate California Penal Code section 311.11, as well as other State and Federal statutes. Disclosure of this information in the designated portion would compromise the investigation of these crimes as it would alert suspect(s) and allow suspect(s) knowledge of evidence that could be destroyed of obfuscated.

Sealing Of Statement of Probable Cause / Affidavit - Child Pornography--Affidavit

Based upon your Affiant's training, experience and conversations that your Affiant had with other Law Enforcement Officers and/or reports that your Affiant has read, your Affiant knows that the entire or designated portion of this Statement of Probable Cause / Affidavit used to support this Search Warrant should be sealed by Court Order until further order by court. The designated material is material that if possessed by Non-Law Enforcement personnel would violate California Penal Code section 311.11, as well as other State and Federal statutes. Disclosure of this information in the designated portion would compromise the investigation of these crimes as it would alert suspect(s) and allow suspect(s) knowledge of evidence that could be destroyed.

Sealing Order for Statement of Probable Cause / Affidavit of Sexual Assault Victim-Search Warrant

IT IS HEREBY ORDERED, that the entire Statement of Probable Cause / Affidavit used to support this Search Warrant be Sealed until further Order of the Court. This Order is Consistent with Penal Code Section 293.5, which allows a sexual assault victim(s) to maintain privacy and be named as Jane/John Doe, if she/he requests.

Sealing Order for Statement of Probable Cause / Affidavit of Sexual Assault Victim

Based upon your Affiant's training, experience and conversations that your Affiant had with other Law Enforcement Officers and/or reports that your Affiant has read, your Affiant requests that the entire Statement of Probable Cause / Affidavit used to support this Search Warrant be Sealed until further Order Court. This Order is Consistent with Penal Code Section 293.5, which allows a sexual assault victim(s) to maintain privacy and be named as Jane/John Doe, if she/he requests.

Sealing Order - Of Entire Search Warrant-Search Warrant

IT IS HEREBY ORDERED, that this entire Search Warrant and Statement of Probable Cause / Affidavit be sealed because disclosure could irremediably harm the ongoing criminal investigation. In accordance with California Rules of Court Rule 243.1(d), this court finds that:

- There exists an overriding interest that overcomes the right of public access to the record;

- The overriding interest supports the sealed record;

- A substantial probability exists that the overriding interest will be prejudiced if the record is not sealed;

- The proposed sealing order is narrowly tailored;

- No less restrictive means exists to achieve the overriding interest.

Sealing Order - Of Entire Search Warrant-Affidavit

Based upon your Affiant's training, experience and conversations that your Affiant had with other Law Enforcement Officers and/or reports that your Affiant has read, your Affiant requests that this entire Search Warrant and Statement of Probable Cause / Affidavit be sealed because disclosure could irremediably harm the ongoing criminal investigation, in accordance with California Rules of Court Rule 243.1(d).

Extension Date of Return to Search Warrant-Search Warrant

IT IS HEREBY ORDERED, based upon the showing in the Statement of Probable Cause / Affidavit by your Affiant (Affiant's name), that it reasonably appears necessary to extend the time for Return to Search Warrant for (number of days) days to (date extended to), (year).

Extension Date of Return to Search Warrant-Affidavit

Based upon your Affiant's training, experience and conversations that your Affiant had with other Law Enforcement Officers and/or reports that your Affiant has read, your Affiant requests that it is necessary to extend the time for Return to Search Warrant for (number of days) days to (date extended to), (year). (Justify reason for extension).

Release of Evidence during the Search Warrant Service-Search Warrant

IT IS HEREBY ORDERED, that the Peace Officers serving the Search Warrant are authorized, without necessity of further Court Order, to return seized items to any known victim(s) if such items have been photographically documented at the site of the Search Warrant service.

Release of Evidence during the Search Warrant Service

Based upon your Affiant's training, experience and conversations that your Affiant had with other Law Enforcement Officers and/or reports that your Affiant has read, your Affiant knows that the Peace Officers serving the Search Warrant should be authorized, without necessity of further Court Order, to return seized items to any known victim(s), if such items have been photographically documented. This allows for the victim(s) to immediately receive the evidence and prevents the booking of the evidence at the Police Agency. The items of evidence are sometimes very large, like furniture, this allows the release of the evidence at the location of the Search Warrant.

Night Time Service - Suspect Arrested – Justification-Affidavit

Based upon your Affiant's training, experience and conversations that your Affiant had with other Law Enforcement Officers and/or reports that your Affiant has read, your Affiant requests this Search Warrant be endorsed for night time service based upon the information set forth herein and your Affiant's experience in the past that when a suspect is arrested for a felony crime he will attempt to notify co-conspirators, friends and associates immediately so that they can destroy, secrete, or dispose of stolen property and other items of evidence which can be used against him/her. It is likely that the fact of the arrest will become known quickly either as a result of the arrestee's disappearance or the arrestee's two authorized telephone calls at booking. In view of these facts, it is your Affiant's opinion that this Search Warrant must be served as soon as possible, before the arrest becomes known and the items sought are destroyed, disposed of, or concealed.

Night Time Service – Suspect Aware Of Investigation-Affidavit

Based upon your Affiant's training, experience and conversations that your Affiant had with other Law Enforcement Officers and/or reports that your Affiant has read, your Affiant requests this Search Warrant be endorsed for night time service based upon the information set forth herein and your Affiant's knowledge that suspect is aware of the ongoing investigation. Based on the suspect's knowledge of the investigation I believe he/she may attempt to, and possibly with the help of co-conspirators, friends and associates attempt to destroy, secrete, or dispose of stolen property and other items of evidence which can be used against him/her. In view of these facts, it is your Affiant's opinion that this Search Warrant must be served as soon as possible, before the suspect or his co-conspirators, friends, and associates, destroy, dispose of, or conceal the items sought within the search warrant.

Night Time Service – Crime Occurs At Night-Affidavit

I request this search warrant be endorsed for nighttime service based upon all the information set forth in this affidavit and the following: My investigation in this case has shown that the methamphetamine sales have taken place all hours of the day and night, including between 10:00 PM and 7:00 AM. To make the strongest possible case, this warrant should be served when methamphetamine sales are in fact taking place at the location to be searched, which includes the hours between 10:00 PM and 7:00 AM

Night Time Service - Premises Unoccupied – Justification-Affidavit

Based upon your Affiant's training, experience and conversations that your Affiant had with other Law Enforcement Officers and/or reports that your Affiant has read, your Affiant requests this Search Warrant be endorsed for night time service based upon the facts set forth above and the following: Following the arrests of the occupant(s) of the premises, peace officers / police officers remained within the premises in order to prevent friends and associates of the occupant(s) from entering and disposing of or destroying the evidence and/or stolen property and/or other items sought. Since no purpose would be served by requiring the officers to wait within the now otherwise unoccupied premises until 7:00 a.m., and since the risk of a confrontation increases if friends or associates of the arrestee(s) come to the premises to dispose of items, your Affiant requests an endorsement permitting search during the night time hours.

9 798476 146346